LONDON BOROUGH OF ENFIELD
LIBRARY SERVICES

This book to be RETURNED on or before the latest date stamped unless a renewal has been obtained by personal call or post, quoting the above number and the date due for return.

EFFECTIVE ADVERTISING

The *Daily Telegraph* Guide for the Small Business

H C Carter

Author's Note

The names of companies and brands and the various products and services and their attributes used for examples in this book are purely imaginary. No reference to past or present companies or products is intended. Product specifications are also imaginary and have no technical merit.

Acknowledgements

I am most grateful to insurance brokers, Godwins (South West) Limited of Plymouth and cinema advertising contractors, Pearl and Dean Limited of London for the technical advice needed to complete parts of this book.

First published in Great Britain in 1986
by Kogan Page Ltd, 120 Pentonville Road, London N1 9JN

British Library Cataloguing in Publication Data

Carter, H.C.
Effective advertising for the small business.
1. Advertising
I. Title
659.1 HF5823
ISBN 1-85091-006-5 Hbk
ISBN 1-85091-007-3 Pbk

Filmset by Mayhew Typesetting, Bristol, England
Printed and bound in Great Britain by
Billing & Sons Limited, Worcester

Contents

Prologue

When an enterprising stallholder in your local market seeks extra business he is unlikely just to stand there and wait anxiously for customers. He displays large and colourful price tickets which point to the best bargains; he places the most attractive goods at the front of the stall to catch the eye of casual shoppers; and then, almost certainly, he will draw attention to his stock with glib or humorous patter.

In other words, the stallholder is making known or advertising, and without it his turnover would certainly drop. Not content to remain passive, he wins extra sales by means of colour, sensible presentation and vocal encouragement.

If the trader has a pleasing personality and takes care to produce an amusing 'script', passers-by will enjoy the entertainment and he will eventually be recognised as a local character. Provided the merchandise on offer is good value for money, he will succeed because he is well known and trusted.

From these street market practices the proprietor or sales director of a small business has much to learn, for here is selling in its most elementary form. By keeping in touch with such basic methods and avoiding the temptation to complicate what are really very simple principles, he or she will escape many of the traps so commonly encountered by those who market their wares in every trade and industry. Of course it is important to consider how to 'make known' a product or service most effectively so that the right people are addressed most persuasively at the lowest cost. But the underlying principles are always as easy to understand as that.

So when you, personally, are confronted by what appears to be a highly complex advertising problem, keep an eye on reality: take a stroll through your nearest market and see how the stallholders might solve it. You are more likely to find an answer there than in the abstract offerings of a formal textbook.

Listen, also, to what ordinary people claim and say in the market, for here is the place to find a truly remarkable slogan.

Foreword

Few businesses today can prosper without advertising in some form. For the large companies, with specialists on the staff and an advertising agency in support, various duties are easily delegated to exactly the right people. Many national advertisers spend millions of pounds each year, and they will happily risk vast sums on launching new brands or services.

In contrast, a small concern must secure the utmost advantage from every penny allocated to publicity. Indeed, during the early stages of development, when professional help is beyond its pocket, the proprietor or sales director must undertake on a miniature scale all the tasks performed by experts in the large business and its agency. He, or she, must become an advertising executive, media planner, copywriter, art buyer, print buyer, print and press production controller, direct mail specialist, display manager and more.

Inevitably, in most cases the results they achieve are disappointing.

Here, then, is a book to escort them along more effective paths until skilled guidance, in the form of an advertising consultant or agent, can be afforded. Afterwards, the advice it contains will help readers appreciate the problems that face a modern agency and so promote a closer understanding from which both parties will benefit.

During my many years in advertising and allied spheres I have been bombarded by colleagues, clients and acquaintances with the most horrifying jargon. This, for the sake of clarity and good manners, I have tried to discard in the writing. Inevitably I shall be accused of over-simplification by those who believe that elementary ideas are best conveyed by fashionable gibberish. Throughout the book, too, I have been at pains to eliminate much detail which, while it might fascinate the specialist, would perhaps confuse those who merely seek practical instruction.

For these reasons my choice of topics has been restricted to the essential and explained as clearly as I can manage with the help of examples. Much of the counsel is easily absorbed and will be regarded by some as obvious even to the beginner. In reply, I need only point to almost any assembly of advertisements to prove them wrong.

When compressing so much information into so few pages it is impossible to arrive at a completely satisfactory arrangement of chapters. Should budgets and campaign planning be placed in their logical position next to the role of advertising in a marketing strategy? If so, how can a reader appreciate the principles involved until he knows something of, say, media selection or the use of direct mail? On the other hand, it is important to see every activity as part of an integrated operation, each supporting the other, and to realise this at an early stage.

Perhaps those who can muster the time and stamina to read the book, or parts of it, a second time will grasp the fundamentals more securely.

Finally, since the techniques and difficulties of advertising in overseas markets are so varied, the subject has been completely excluded. Readers who need help in this field will be wise to consult a British agency with suitable experience, and preferably also associates, in the countries concerned.

An apology

In this book, for the sake of brevity and with regard to good sense, I have commonly classified readers, advertisers and others as male. For any offence so caused I most sincerely apologise.

In fact the advertising business has for many years recognised the equal abilities of women. Throughout the industry, and particularly in agencies, women occupy executive and senior positions alongside their male colleagues. Without their skills and expertise we would be very much poorer.

H C Carter
June 1985

Part 1

First Considerations

Chapter 1

What Advertising Can Do for the Small Business

For some businesses advertising is a vital tool, while in others it may be quite unnecessary. For example, if you decide to sell a product by mail order a platform of some kind, such as a sales letter or press advertisement, is required. On the other hand, if you provide a service to just two or three customers and are already working for them seven days a week, you would have no reason for advertising your services. Note, however, that if you eventually employ an assistant and need extra work to keep him or her fully occupied, you may decide at that stage to advertise on a modest scale.

Between these extremes, advertising can be used to perform a number of tasks:

1. To aid recognition of and build confidence in a product or service wherever it is sold.
2. To gain acceptance of a product by wholesalers, retailers and consumers, and thus help to achieve distribution.
3. To stimulate demand for a specific brand.
4. To counter competing brands.
5. To counter the effects of seasonal demand.
6. To launch a new product or service more quickly.
7. To promote a completely new idea or method.
8. To increase sales and thereby gain the advantages of greater or mass production.
9. To produce enquiries and reduce or obviate the need for cold canvassing.
10. To increase the salesman's confidence.
11. To introduce a new pack or a modified or improved product or service.
12. To announce a special bargain or offer.
13. To explain a new product or service.
14. To increase retail turnover and make money invested in stock work harder.
15. To improve or change a reputation or concept.
16. To encourage prospects to visit a showroom or store.

Plainly, advertising has many functions, but before resolving to use it in some form the businessman must first define as accurately as possible the main reasons for doing so and be quite clear about the results he wants to achieve. Let us examine some examples:

☐ A retailer, Mr XYZ, who sells art materials and related products, is appointed the area agent for a new instant lettering system. Previously his customers have been mainly amateur and professional artists and a few commercial art studios and drawing offices. Now his market is increased to include a large number of businesses within a 15-mile radius of his premises. Before deciding how to approach these new prospects he must first ask himself whether advertising will be the best way of doing so. Obviously a salesman or telephone canvasser would take months to speak to them all. Window displays will be valuable, and catalogues can be sent to existing customers. But to make an immediate impact and then remind people time and again, advertising must surely be the most effective means.

There will also be some incidental advantages. When new or existing customers need instant lettering sheets they will probably order other lines at the same time, and for important buyers it may pay the retailer to offer a delivery service. His advertisements will also reach and influence artists who for one reason or another have not dealt with him in the past.

We shall follow the subsequent action and progress of Mr XYZ in Chapter 7.

☐ Two partners, with a small staff, have been making chairs, settees and stools of excellent quality in a variety of designs. Their main outlets are a number of London stores. Having moved to new premises in the outer suburbs, the partners decide to increase their output and they must therefore seek new stockists within a 50-mile radius of their works. They have approached several stores in the district, but most of them are much smaller than the London establishments and have asked whether the products will be advertised.

The partners now appreciate the role that advertising can play in achieving distribution. But after some consideration they also realise that it will give them greater control over the selling process. With the help of sales leaflets in full colour they can show their furniture in idealistic surroundings, while press advertisements can perhaps illustrate husband and wife enjoying the pleasure of new acquisitions for their home.

Here are powerful reasons for advertising.

☐ A small company is producing taps of a completely new design which, by a patented process, save up to 50 per cent of the running hot water used when washing hands in factory and office lavatories. Research has shown that in nearly 90 per cent of cases running water is used in preference to filling the bowl. Once the taps are fitted they save enormous sums of money in a year, but persuading companies and institutions to investigate the benefits is proving difficult.

Once again we find excellent reasons for advertising: architects and other specifiers should be encouraged to install the device in new or renovated buildings, while energy managers and similar executives must be persuaded to replace existing taps. Only a carefully planned campaign can reach enough prospects to stimulate interest and demand quickly and on a suitable scale.

From this introduction you will begin to understand that advertising is more than just a crude means of increasing sales. For many firms it plays an important part in their marketing strategy. This role we shall examine in the next chapter.

Chapter 2

The Role of Advertising in a Marketing Strategy

What do we mean by marketing? *Selling in a market* is perhaps an absurd simplification, but I think we can reasonably say that, in essence, marketing is the whole process of distributing a product or providing a service, from the moment it is made or is available in the factory or office until it reaches the eventual user.

The marketing process involves or may require a study of research, creating and satisfying demand, competition, channels of distribution such as wholesalers, retailers or factors, market locations at home and overseas, packaging, handling, transport, storage and, of course, selling techniques. Every one of these subjects may have some bearing on advertising methods, while conversely, advertising needs may influence almost any aspect of marketing. Here are some examples:

- The inventor of a new novel product for use by the general public believes it has very great sales potential, and he therefore wants to maintain complete control over manufacturing and marketing. Because he can afford to do so only on a restricted scale, he selects a number of 'test' towns within easy reach of his factory to assess attitudes and likely demand.

  He immediately realises that advertising needs will have an important bearing on his general marketing strategy, since although wholesalers are not interested in handling his product, retailers seem willing to stock and display the line provided interest is stimulated by advertising. The most appropriate medium is the local press, and he soon discovers that one group of weekly newspapers plus a regional daily cover many of the towns in which he seeks retail distribution. By concentrating his efforts in the areas in which these newspapers circulate and repeating his sales message in the local and regional press week after week, he can publicise the product more effectively at lower cost.

  Thus, advertising tactics have influenced the marketing plan.

- Because modern cars are very reliable and service intervals are now so long, the proprietor of a small but efficient repair and maintenance shop is finding that much of his work is now on older models. Because owners often cannot afford the extensive attention required to make such vehicles roadworthy, the proprietor is becoming increasingly worried and frustrated. He therefore decides to seek new sources of business, including maintenance contracts with companies in his immediate area, particularly those with small fleets of salesmen's cars or taxis.

He wants to emphasise the skilled, trustworthy and conscientious service he and his staff can offer and his willingness to deal promptly with emergencies — even to the extent of working overnight if necessary. No other garages in the district can match this flexible and personal attention to individual problems.

Because he prefers to supervise all the major jobs in progress, the proprietor's time is limited, and in any case he is not happy about making cold calls. A flow of serious enquiries from the right kind of prospects would seem to be the ideal answer to this particular marketing problem and, as we shall learn in later chapters, direct mail advertising is the obvious medium to use, supported perhaps by advertisements in local journals that are read by business people.

☐ A small retailer dealing in general hardware, gardening accessories and DIY products has decided to change radically his marketing policy. For the past five years he has operated in a conventional way, offering a few special bargains and maintaining price levels on the rest of his stock at or around those recommended by the manufacturers. Customers have enjoyed personal attention at the counter, but because of intense local competition this standard of service is now much too expensive in relation to sales.

Turnover in the last accounting year dropped slightly, while prices rose. He therefore makes the following changes:

(a) Sluggish lines will be shed as quickly as possible at sale prices.
(b) Counters will be replaced by self-service fittings.
(c) Staff will be reduced to comprise a full-time assistant and two self-employed part-timers to help during busy periods.
(d) There will be a modern check-out system.
(e) He will increasingly deal in job lots and special purchases, such as liquidation stocks, where he can buy reasonable quality at extremely low prices for cash.

The success of this transformation will depend very largely upon advertising effectively within the restrictions of a budget that must be fixed quite arbitrarily before the changes are made, and without the benefit of experience in the new style of publicity which will be needed to promote the revised trading policy. There can be little doubt, however, that a combination of low prices and aggressive trading will attract many more customers and it will be an easy task to adjust the advertising outlay accordingly.

In these three cases the proprietors have prepared logical and sensible schemes in which the role of advertising is sharply defined during the first stages of planning. There are many similar instances in the chapters to follow.

We have already seen in Chapter 1 some of the functions that advertising can perform. Now we perceive, too, the importance of including it in the initial marketing strategy and deciding how extensively it will be used. Clearly, then, budgets and campaign planning must be considered next.

Chapter 3

Budgets and Campaign Planning

The discipline of preparing an annual budget for a firm has many advantages, but is particularly valuable when planning marketing activities for the year ahead.

First, the businessman must normally consider the many possibilities and try to picture the most favourable and then the most difficult circumstances he is likely to encounter, bearing in mind the many factors which may affect his company. Between these extremes he can imagine a middle course on which his calculations may be based.

Usually he will list the turnover he expects to achieve month by month or client by client in order to assemble a sales forecast. Against this he can weigh the estimated expenses and so reach a target figure for profits.

From such preliminaries he will be able to sketch his marketing plan for the year to come. Perhaps, for example, the business is seasonal and he will imagine a sales chart with sharp peaks in, say, March and December unless action is taken to improve turnover during the quieter months. He may believe that sales will steadily accelerate throughout the first six months but then reach a plateau unless a new salesman is taken on in April. Perhaps he knows that an important contract will end in August and he must somehow replace the business before then.

From this picture, however blurred, will spring reasons and a tentative pattern for the year's advertising. Of course, research may also influence this initial review very strongly, but because it is so specialised readers are advised to consult suitable books on the subject.

Even if he takes advertisement space regularly in certain periodicals or newspapers, the marketing director should always challenge this procedure at budget time and ask himself whether last year's plan is likely to be the most effective in the months to come or if a change in policy will yield better results. Markets and the media that serve them are rarely so stable that an advertising campaign can be repeated without a review.

After deciding on the objectives of a forthcoming advertising programme it is necessary to establish how much money must be spent to achieve them. To start with, it is often most convenient to express that sum as a fraction of the sales turnover. For instance, if you are selling by mail order your advertising costs might be 10 per cent of your gross sales or even higher. In contrast, a manufacturer with an order book that is full for the year ahead could decide to advertise only occasionally in his main industrial journal in order to maintain enquiries for capacity in, say, a year's time. His advertising budget might therefore be as low as ½ per cent, perhaps with a contingency sum in hand lest current orders are cancelled for unforeseen reasons.

Most business people will find, however, that between 1 and 3 per cent of turnover is an appropriate budget. But having decided on a provisional sum, it is then essential to prepare an outline plan of campaign to see whether the appropriation is realistic or too generous.

Planning and costing your campaign

Now you need to define the practical purposes of your advertising in as much detail as you can and decide upon your solutions to the problems involved. Naturally, these will be far from precise, but they will at least guide you towards realistic figures and demonstrate the approximate outlay required.

Later chapters deal with media selection, advertisement production and the many other functions which influence the cost of a campaign. You must, obviously, be reasonably conversant with these subjects before attempting to produce a practical scheme. For the present, however, it will suffice to understand the elementary considerations likely to affect your plan and therefore your costs. They include the following measures:

Define and pinpoint the markets and people you are trying to reach and influence
In some cases this will be immediately apparent, in others more difficult. For example:

(a) A firm that deals in farm implements can define its market exactly. It knows the name and address of every farmer within the area it serves, and will quickly learn about newcomers who, in most instances, will simply replace farmers leaving the region or retiring.

(b) If the same firm accepts the agency for a new ride-on mower, it can still define its market easily but will have considerable difficulty in listing the owners — private, commercial or institutional — of every property in its area with grounds of, say, an acre or more.

(c) When the firm extends its activities into selling smaller mowers the market becomes virtually impossible to pinpoint with accuracy, since it consists of every property with a lawn or rough grass.

Here it is important to note that if you are selling to the general public it may be necessary to take account of the social status and income brackets of the people most likely to be interested in your product or service.

Define the advertising medium likely to reach these prospects most effectively at lowest cost

In the case of (a) above, the firm has an accurate list of farmers and can therefore mail them at low cost as often as it wishes. There will be very little waste circulation.

In (b), however, it is impossible to reach prospects without significant waste. House-to-house circulars in districts where properties have large gardens may be one solution, but in remote rural areas the expense would probably be prohibitive. It might be cheaper to mail properties in likely districts. Alternatively, prospects might be reached more economically by taking space in local magazines read mainly by more affluent families in rural areas, or in suitable local newspapers.

In (c), the firm's market is virtually every family apart from those who live in homes without gardens. Approaching them by direct mail would be much too expensive, but house-to-house distribution, press, radio or television might be suitable for covering this mass market.

Assess the cost of using this main medium during the year

A fundamental rule of advertising is that your message must be repeated as often as possible to the same group of people. Even if you book a full-page space in a periodical or local newspaper, it would be unsafe to assume that the majority of readers are aware of your claims or product after just one insertion. In fact you are more likely to achieve recognition and awareness of your name or brand and the benefits associated with it by booking a series of smaller spaces in succeeding issues of the same publication.

From this it follows that the effectiveness of your advertising is not always directly related to the amount of money you spend.

The size of your space or the length of your radio or television message should be determined by what you need to say, your means of attracting attention and then holding prospects' interest.

From this simple statement you might gather that those who book huge spaces in the national press in order to convey a very simple message are wasting large sums of money, and I would agree this is sometimes true.

If you are introducing a new product or service, large spaces or long commercials may be essential to explain and illustrate the benefits. On the other hand, small spaces and brief commercials are often adequate for simple reminder advertisements designed to aid recognition of a brand or name and encourage an association of ideas by means of a catch-line or slogan.

When launching a new product or service on a limited budget, a combination of long advertisements to explain, and brief ones to remind is often a good answer.

Colour is another factor to be debated. Ask yourself whether it is absolutely vital or merely desirable. For example, when planning a direct mail advertising campaign for a range of bathroom fittings in various colours, the illustrations must obviously be in full colour; but advertisements in local magazines inviting readers to visit the showrooms or send for literature would work perfectly well in black and white.

Assess the cost of supporting media

Another basic rule of campaign planning is that the main advertising medium should be supported by messages in other media wherever possible. The effectiveness of direct mail shots to industrial or trade buyers can be improved by reminders in appropriate journals. Press advertising to the public can be reinforced by poster or radio advertising or house-to-house circulars.

In many cases further support can be given at exhibitions, in showrooms, window displays, van designs and by car stickers. Main selling points, themes or slogans should be repeated whenever appropriate in sales literature, catalogues, instruction booklets and data sheets.

Assess the cost of producing your advertisements

Never waste good money spent on advertisement space, radio or television time or direct mail postage by saving a few pounds on a low standard of presentation. The subject is discussed at length in future chapters, and having read them you will be able to estimate production costs more accurately. It may help you to know, however, that the professionals prefer to allocate 15 per cent of the cost of press space for insertions in black and white or 25 per cent for colour. But in essence these figures are merely an approximate guide. Much will depend upon the amount you spend on space, the size of your advertisements and their contents.

For direct mail it is a simple matter to calculate the cost of postage, while quotations for stationery, printing and handling will be submitted by your suppliers. Similarly, television or radio contractors, printers and others will gladly help you calculate rough costs for budget purposes.

Assess the cost of related material or activities

Even if you have a separate allocation for such items as exhibitions and literature, it is important to assess their costs in parallel with the advertising appropriation because the activities and material are closely related in so many ways.

At this stage it is necessary only to appreciate the importance of preparing realistic forecasts based on a provisional plan of campaign. Precise costs will emerge when the media programme and other elements in the scheme are examined in detail. Before reaching firm decisions on such matters, however, it is essential to consider the campaign theme since it will affect the size of the spaces to be booked, the length of radio or television commercials, the design of sales literature and many similar subjects.

Chapter 4

Campaign Themes and Slogans

Now we approach the problem of how to devise our basic message: that is, the fundamental idea or ideas we wish to impart and, equally important, what action we want prospects to take in our favour. Such action can be as positive as sending an order — which may require a coupon — or as nebulous as thinking well of a service or product so that it will either be accepted when offered or selected in preference to others in the market.

The message

In the previous chapter it was said that your message must be repeated as often as possible to the same group of people. This principle of repetition extends to the message itself, since a variety of major statements simply weakens the campaign's effectiveness. You should understand that, although you live daily with your product or service and are exuberant about its every feature, the average potential customer is unlikely to feel even the slightest enthusiasm for it and certainly will not memorise a list of advantages. In truth, if, during the early stages of a product being launched, a large number of prospects remember its name and associate with it just one outstanding fact, you will have achieved a great deal.

This is not to say that you should confine your message to one main advantage. Obviously you can list several. But by deciding on a theme and finding angles that lead to that central idea, you will greatly strengthen the campaign's impact. If this chief concept can be expressed as a slogan that is original, distinctive and easy to remember, you will gain considerable extra benefits. Let us take an example:

A firm trading in a large town with heavily populated areas within a 10-mile radius sells a completely new glazing system with the following characteristics:

1. Frames in white pvc are reinforced by a patented process which allows the widths and thicknesses of glazing bars and surrounds to be reduced to those of timber or metal units.

2. This removes one of the main objections to pvc windows, which are often ugly, especially in smaller sizes, because the frames are so wide.
3. No condensation on pvc frames.
4. Immensely strong.
5. Improved insulation.
6. Cannot rot, warp or twist.
7. Surface chips virtually unnoticeable.
8. Purpose-made to fit any opening.
9. No maintenance.
10. All the usual benefits of other double glazing systems.

The sales director can explain and illustrate every one of these advantages in his literature, but in common with all window specialists he has three main problems to solve in his approach to this crowded market:

(a) How can his firm establish an individual and easily recognisable character?
(b) How can he quickly establish a reputation for reliability?
(c) How can he produce a steady flow of enquiries?

After the company has traded for a year or so it will begin to build a good name and so gain a certain amount of business from recommendations. Meanwhile, apart from laborious cold canvassing, advertising will be its only means of entering the market. However, the director has one very powerful selling argument in that the pvc frames are neither wider nor thicker than aluminium ones and will not 'sweat' with condensation. Other selling points, although useful, are relatively unimportant. His principal advertising medium will be the local weekly newspaper, supported by house-to-house circulars.

Logically, then, his campaign theme will be summarised in the headline, 'Unbelievably narrow. Unbelievably thin. Unbelievably strong.' This will be buttressed by good illustrations and the slogan 'Seeing's believing', with an invitation to visit the showrooms. The text in the press advertisement would introduce subsidiary advantages, and by repeating this one message regularly in the local press, he would ensure that even those readers who were not at that time interested in replacement windows would eventually associate the company with this specific benefit.

If the headline and slogan were varied at intervals, readers might be confused, perhaps remembering the company but failing to connect it with the outstanding advantages of the pvc frames. It might seem to be just another glazing firm instead of the only local business with something unique to offer in this field.

Without doubt, it is wise to define in clear and basic terms the theme of a new campaign during the early stages of planning. Apart from sharpening your thoughts on the creative approach, it produces, too, a more accurate idea of the size of the space needed to accommodate a sales message or the length of a radio or television commercial.

Checklist

1. Is it likely that advertising in some form will add impetus to your marketing effort?
2. Is advertising absolutely vital, extremely important or merely desirable?
3. What role or roles will it play?
4. Is your advertising allocation for the financial year realistic?
5. Have you mapped out a rough campaign, based on the cost of media, number of insertions and production costs?
6. Have you considered press, radio, television, cinema, posters, direct mail, house-to-house?
7. Have you allowed for the expense of supporting activities and material such as literature, display pieces, exhibitions, salesmen's portfolios or van design?
8. Have you devoted serious thought to your campaign theme?
9. Will a slogan be valuable? If so, have you spent enough time on finding some preliminary ideas?

Author's note: Read the remaining chapters of this book and then return to this first part before attempting to prepare your budget. Every subject in the book has an important bearing on your detailed programme.

Part 2

Press Advertising

Chapter 5

Selecting the Right Publications

In order to select the most suitable publications for a press campaign it is necessary to assemble for consideration a list of every newspaper and periodical likely to reach the desired group of prospects. In some cases this will be easy, in others very complex.

Let us consider three typical examples:

☐ The proprietor of a delicatessen in a large town stocks a wide range of food products unobtainable elsewhere within about ten miles. His catchment area is therefore very accurately defined. Except in rare instances, customers are unlikely to travel more than about six miles to buy from him, and the town's local newspapers and magazines are thus the only publications it would be sensible to use.

☐ A company has the sole agency in Somerset, Devon and Cornwall for a new, low-cost copying machine. It will interest thousands of small businesses and professional people throughout the region. In this case the marketing director must consider the following publications:

(a) Local magazines, particularly those published specifically for business people.
(b) Weekly newspapers, including those distributed free, and regional Sundays.
(c) Regional daily newspapers, including evenings.
(d) Miscellaneous periodicals, such as chamber of commerce newsletters.

☐ An investment adviser specialises in certain kinds of bonds and unit trusts offered to the general public by large financial institutions. Although his office is in a provincial city, his market embraces the whole of the UK. The advertising media he must consider therefore include:

(a) Local publications likely to be read by people with money to invest. The big advantage of building a local clientele is the ease of visiting them for discussions, and the low cost of reaching them by car or telephone.

(b) Every newspaper and periodical throughout the UK which is read by large numbers of prospects with, say, £10,000 or more to save.

(c) Every periodical published specifically for investors.

In this example the investment adviser must conduct extensive research into the various publications available to establish the 'best buys', but even then the choice is so wide that he can never be absolutely sure his selections will pull sound enquiries at the lowest possible cost. By adopting the procedures described in this and following chapters, however, the risk of serious failure is much reduced.

At this stage we are concerned only with finding the most suitable publications; other considerations, such as classified or display positions, size of space, frequency of insertion, colour and their effect on costs and buying decisions are examined in Chapter 6.

Define the target audience

The first step in the selection process is to define as accurately as you can the people or firms you want to reach and influence, and then list the publications of all kinds that they are likely to read. As we have seen, sometimes this is a simple task, producing perhaps a dozen or less titles. But in many cases it may be necessary initially to categorise them by groups such as motor cycling magazines, medical journals, electronics periodicals or daily newspapers published in certain regions. Some campaigns may involve the definition of two or more groups. For instance, the launch of a new product might require a series of advertisements in the trade press to encourage orders from wholesalers or retailers prior to advertisements appearing in selected newspapers and magazines to create demand from the general public.

Investigate the available publications

Having listed every publication likely to be of value, certain essential facts about each must then be determined. Some of this information is available from press directories in the public library, but the easiest method is to consult *British Rate & Data*,* usually called *BRAD*. This monthly reference work lists the vast majority of

*Maclean Hunter Ltd, 76 Oxford Street, London W1N 0HH.

newspapers and periodicals in the UK, and gives their advertisement rates, technical data and many other facts, including circulation figures. Moreover, publications are arranged in consumer and business categories, so that finding the journals which reach a specific classification, such as amateur photographers or nurses, is quick and easy. *BRAD* is equally valuable for tracing and evaluating national, regional and local newspapers, including those distributed free of charge.

Of course, business people are usually conversant with the main journals circulating in their own trades or industries. Surprisingly, however, they occasionally have illogical prejudices or criticisms which can only be disproved by unbiased analysis. Furthermore, many firms sell their products or services to groups of consumers, institutions or companies unconnected with their industries, and must therefore investigate the appropriate publications with care. The proprietor of a factory that is about to produce flexible tubing for glasshouse irrigation systems will probably know every journal read by the plastics industry, but is most unlikely to be so familiar with the merits of the several publications taken by growers. For him, *BRAD* will be a prime source of information.

Initial investigation and analysis requires a study of the following factors:

1. Editorial content and its value

This is a matter for personal judgement, but authoritative articles and comment are usually easy to recognise, and by reading some of the more important features in two or three recent issues you can normally judge whether such material is likely to interest your prospects.

2. Circulation

There are two main types of circulation to consider: either net sales or the number distributed free of charge to particular groups of readers.

In some cases circulation figures are verified by an independent body, such as the Audit Bureau of Circulations (ABC), and they are therefore entirely dependable. Otherwise you must gauge for yourself the reliability of the publishers' own statements.

Apart from circulation figures, the nature and quality of a readership is important. For example, a weekly newspaper with net sales of 10,000 copies may seem to compare badly with the claimed 40,000 copies of a newspaper distributed free of charge in the same district. Investigation might show, however, that whereas the latter contains very little editorial matter and is therefore discarded by the average household within a few hours of receipt, its rival has many pages of news, articles and useful information, and is kept for a full six days, during which it may be read on two or three occasions by every member of the family.

Note, too, that readers usually place greater value on a publication they must buy.

3. Readers

In many groups of publications the advertiser can select either mass circulations or more closely defined readerships. The tabloid national newspapers, for instance, offer very large net sales of three or four millions; in general, however, the readers have very different attitudes, tastes and needs from those who regularly take the quality nationals, which may have circulations of little more than a quarter of a million. But you should also remember that nowadays income is not always an accurate guide to social class.

The importance of readership studies applies equally to trade, industrial and professional publications. For example, medical journals with a general appeal may reach 60,000 or more doctors, whereas a periodical devoted to a highly specialised medical subject may be read by less than a thousand — who could be exactly the people you want to reach.

This variety of choice within specific groups of publications is of enormous benefit to advertisers, enabling them to focus a message on carefully defined prospects and thus avoiding waste circulation.

4. Costs: a standard for comparisons

As you will have realised by now, assessing the merits of publications for a forthcoming campaign relies very largely on perception and common sense. There is, however, a mathematical method of comparison which is always useful in the preliminary planning. By taking a publication's net sales figure and the cost of a page advertisement, one arrives at the 'cost per thousand readers' via a simple formula:

$$\text{Cost per page} \quad \text{divided by} \quad \frac{\text{net sales}}{1{,}000}$$

So, for example, if a journal with a circulation (net sales) of 100,000 charges £500 for a page advertisement, the cost per thousand readers is

$$£500 \quad \text{divided by} \quad \frac{100{,}000}{1{,}000} \quad \text{or } £5.$$

But this cannot always give a truly accurate guide because page sizes vary and an advertisement of dimensions that fit, say, publications of A4 size will be very much more prominent — and thus probably more effective — in these journals than in tabloid publications. Even if a comparison is based on the cost of an A4 space in the latter it may still be unfair.

5. Frequency of publication

A daily paper is discarded in less than 24 hours. A local weekly newspaper or a weekly journal is often referred to several times and may be kept for seven days. Monthly or quarterly magazines have an even longer life and may be saved in a collection for many years.

Dailies are less likely to be read by several members of a family than are weekly newspapers, although evenings are often referred to regularly for the television programmes. Weekly, monthly or quarterly magazines are sometimes read by families and then passed on to friends.

On the other hand, dailies allow you to publish an advertisement on a specific day and enable you to repeat your message several times in one week. Additionally, they can impart a sense of news and urgency, and because they are thrown out so quickly they encourage readers to fill in a coupon immediately or act at once.

Frequency, then, is an important factor to be taken into account when planning a campaign. Dailies or weeklies can obviously be used for instant impact and to suggest topicality. But in addition to an initial value, monthlies or quarterlies may have a long-term reminder role.

The benefits of annual publications and year books are debatable. Perhaps the best rule is to take space only in those which you know are constantly used for reference, but even then you must ensure your advertisement appears in exactly the right position, next to suitable editorial matter.

6. Colour

The use of full colour processes in advertisements to reproduce photographs, drawings or transparencies, is extremely expensive but in special circumstances may be justified. Sometimes it will be more economical to publish an advertisement in monotone urging readers to send for your colour literature.

If, however, you are intent on using full colour in a trade or technical journal it will pay to investigate the cost of having your own colour leaflet or folder bound in. Alternatively, most journals will accept loose inserts, which can also be printed by your own supplier and may serve a dual purpose since they, too, can be used as sales literature.

Apart from full colour advertisements, you can book a page or half-page space in black and a standard second colour, which is usually blue, red or yellow. Using the same colour throughout a campaign attracts greater attention and aids recognition. It can therefore be extremely valuable, and the availability of a certain colour can be an important factor when selecting publications.

Having completed this preliminary review of every publication likely to be useful in a campaign, the advertiser can now select the most suitable, compile a list and take the first steps towards practical space buying.

Checklist

1. Have you defined the group or groups of prospects you want to reach and influence?
2. Have you listed every publication likely to be seen by these people?
3. Have you studied each of these publications and noted
   (a) Editorial contents?
   (b) Circulation (net sales)?
   (c) Types of reader and quality?
   (d) Cost per thousand readers?
   (e) Frequency of publication?
   (f) If applicable, the cost of colour?

Chapter 6

Space Buying

From *BRAD* and other reference books you will find the names and addresses of companies which publish the newspapers and periodicals on your list. Now you can write to the advertisement managers or ring them, asking for specimen copies of the publications under review, the current rate cards and any supporting information that may be available. Remember, you are making your first approach to people who may prove very good friends in the years ahead. As you will see in later chapters, there are many ways in which they can help you, so be pleasant, be reasonable and do not bully.

Make the best use of advertising space

When all the information has arrived you can start your analysis in detail, preferably preparing a chart so that you can easily compare such factors as frequency of publication, circulations and whether or not they are authenticated, page sizes, remarks about editorial content and type or class of reader, plus facts you glean from publishers' literature and rate cards that may affect your decisions. The cost per thousand readers, including the extra expense of position or colour, if required, should be noted prominently against each publication so that it cannot be overlooked. You should then consider the following subjects:

1. Position

The position of an advertisement can make an enormous difference to its effectiveness. For example, a quarter-page space in the back pages of a magazine among a mass of similar advertisements is less likely to be noticed and read than an identical advertisement in a solus position next to important editorial matter.

It has also been shown that the position of an advertisement on a page, and even the page itself, can be of some significance. Many advertisers believe that a top right-hand situation on a right-hand page is ideal, although, of course, the reader's attention will be influenced by many other elements such as surrounding items, the design of an advertisement and the degree of contrast it enjoys with other matter on the page. If, for instance, the page is very crowded with masses of type and heavy illustrations, a panel containing just a few words within generous white borders will attract the eye whatever its position.

A number of publications, particularly trade and technical journals, arrange their format so that advertisements are always next to some kind of editorial content, and in this case there is no extra charge for 'next matter' positions. Similarly, newspaper advertisements often adjoin or are close to editorial columns.

But the proximity of editorial or news matter is not the only factor to be considered. It would be absurd to place an advertisement for a product bought exclusively by women on a newspaper's sports page, which would be read mainly by men. A DIY product would be inappropriate next to an article for children but would be likely to yield good results if it were near a feature on home maintenance.

The position of an advertisement is in many cases so important that careful negotiation with the publishers is essential. There may be an extra charge, but sometimes a good position will be guaranteed as an inducement to book a series at standard or run-of-paper rates. Your advertisements should never be placed among many others at the front or back of a periodical. Make this ban a firm condition of your contract and pay extra if need be for good positions, since you will certainly get much better value for the additional outlay.

Very special positions such as front page solus or on the front cover may be unavailable for many months ahead, with a list of applicants awaiting future vacancies. To book these premium spaces you may need extreme patience; they do, of course, have a prestige and reminder value for those who use them regularly.

2. Classified advertising

Never overlook the benefits of classified advertising. In years gone by these columns were simply continuous and closely set type matter, but with the advent of semi-display boxes an imaginative campaign can now be run in the classified pages. Because publishers accept complete artwork for these spaces there are no restrictions on advertisement design, and for certain products or services very effective advertising programmes in miniature are possible on a small budget.

When selecting publications for your press schedules, always examine the potential that the classified columns may offer, especially for reminder messages.

3. The size of your advertisement

In Chapter 4 I emphasised the importance of defining the theme of your campaign and devoting some thought to the creative approach in order to give you an idea of the size of your advertisements. If, for example, you are launching a new product that requires a detailed explanation of its use or advantages you will need large spaces to convey the full story. If your budget is modest you might, however, reduce costs by booking small spaces or even classifieds to create a desire to know more and then exhorting the reader to call at your showroom, to ring you, to send for a leaflet or visit a local stockist.

Once again I would stress the danger of inserting just one large advertisement in either a periodical or a newspaper. A series of smaller spaces in the same publication will almost certainly yield better results and may even cost you less.

The size of an advertisement is determined by the need for repetition, by your advertising allocation, your sales message, your objective and the action you want prospects to take. Never book advertisement space until you are absolutely sure that your copy will fit snugly into the area available. Too little space would be disastrous, too much would be wasteful.

A glance at the rate cards will give the production details, including type areas. You will see that, apart from pages or double-page spreads, the various advertisement spaces are described either as fractions of a page or in terms of depth and columns. Thus, for example, you might book a 20cm × 2-column space. The sizes of special areas, such as front covers, are also shown in the rate cards.

4. Mechanical production restrictions

Despite attempts at standardisation over the years, there is still a variety of page sizes and column widths. When booking space, therefore, it is advisable to take these dimensions into account. You will learn in Chapter 9 how advertisement copy can be enlarged or reduced in size photographically at low cost.* In contrast, if the dimensions of the space booked do not allow a simple photographic adjustment, an artist must prepare new artwork. This can be extremely expensive when repeated over a number of insertions.

Before booking, check the type areas carefully in conjunction with your artist. He or she will be conversant with the problems and can save you unnecessary expense.

* In the world of advertising and publishing the word 'copy' means text matter or a manuscript or matter to be printed, including artwork.

5. Colour

If you decide to book a standard second colour, or have negotiated a special one, it is important to understand the restrictions of newspaper and periodical production. Printing many thousands of copies within the limitations imposed by a strict deadline precludes meticulous matching, and you cannot reasonably expect great accuracy. Full colour processes are even more vulnerable.

Before booking space in full colour, be sure you have firm quotations for photography, artwork and production costs. It is also essential to ask your artist to ring the various publishers so that he knows exactly what is needed. If in doubt, ask all the publishers concerned to confirm their requirements in writing because there will almost certainly be differences between them due to the diversity of modern reproduction techniques. Be very cautious about this to avoid additional charges from the publisher, the artist, photographer or the platemaker, who may be required to supply sets of positive or negative film.

Further guidance on this subject is given in Chapter 9.

6. Publishers' claims

Having weighed the many factors discussed in these two chapters and analysed all the available information, you should now be able to arrive at firm decisions about which publications to use in your campaign and the size of the spaces to be booked. Before placing orders, however, you should scrutinise publishers' statements and check their validity.

Is the circulation figure certified? If not, why not? If a publication is said to be the official journal of an institution, is the latter properly constituted? Does the publication emanate from a reputable house which issues other well known and reliable titles? Is it professionally produced? Is the editorial matter authentic and carefully presented? How much advertising does the publication carry? Do the advertisers include some nationally recognised names?

If there are free distribution newspapers on your list, have you checked the reliability of their delivery methods? If in doubt, is there a local business friend with experience of advertising in the paper who can tell you about the results he gets?

7. Preparing your provisional press schedule

Investigations completed, you can now prepare a provisional schedule of insertions. As we have seen, frequency is important and in general terms it is better to use smaller spaces where common sense allows. At this stage, too, you can refer to the publishers' rate cards to determine the discounts offered for ordering a series of advertisements. Aim at the ideal schedule and trim the selection if necessary to meet your budget. It is better to concentrate your efforts on a restricted audience rather than scatter them over too many publications.

Having planned a year's campaign the beginner would be most unwise to book all the space at once. Cancellations are accepted provided a specified period of notice is given, but it will be better to test the value of the selected publications over, say, four or six months.

Publishers will always be happy to accept your initial order and 'pencil in' the remaining dates, which can be booked when you have evidence of the publication's power to produce the results you are seeking. Remember to advise the advertisement manager that you will claim the retrospective discounts due to you if the extra space is booked, and note this condition on your order so that there can be no dispute later on.

8. Space booking

The advertisement and editorial staff of every publication connected with your business or fields of activity are valuable allies. The great majority are helpful, friendly and deeply interested in the market you serve. They meet many people, including senior management, and are often a source of authentic information on almost every matter that may affect your aspirations.

When you send for a rate card and other details you can be sure of receiving phone calls or visits from an advertisement representative soon afterwards. No matter how crowded your diary, whatever crisis may have arisen during the day, it will pay you in many ways to be pleasant and diplomatic. If you can establish a rapport with him or her, so much the better. Here is a person who moves daily in circles of great importance to you, has much he can tell you and may even recommend your service or products to others. He also has colleagues in the editorial department who may give you very valuable publicity virtually free of charge. Here is a relationship to nourish! Of course it will not hinder your bargaining keenly for the best positions at lowest cost, and since a representative wants you to get the best possible results from your advertisements and so become a regular client, you will be given the fairest deal he can afford. Listen well to the advice you receive.

Always confirm your bookings with written orders and file away copies for checking the publisher's formal acceptance. You will need them, too, for verifying the invoices, supported by vouchers, that you will eventually receive. Now you can draw up a master schedule of bookings containing the following details:

(a) Name of publication
(b) Circulation
(c) Size of space (eg quarter-page)
(d) Number of insertions
(e) Cost per insertion
(f) Total cost
(g) Dates (or months) of each insertion.

At the same time you should prepare a production schedule giving the 'copy date' for each insertion, a description of the space booked (eg quarter-page), its exact dimensions (known as the type area) and the kind of copy required, such as 'artwork', 'litho negative, 40 screen' or 'letterpress, 48 screen'. Do not be alarmed by these technical terms, which are quite easy to understand and are explained in Chapter 9. Meanwhile, our next task must be to study the many factors which affect the creation of successful advertisements.

Checklist

1. Have you received rate cards and specimen copies?
2. Have you prepared an analysis in chart form?
3. Have you considered position/size/mechanical production problems/colour/publishers' claims/amount of advertising carried/types of advertising carried/publishers' reputations and standards?
4. Have you prepared a provisional schedule after considering frequency/publishers' discounts/adaptation costs?
5. Have you booked only test spaces?
6. Has the publisher 'pencilled in' the remainder?
7. Have you confirmed your orders in writing?
8. Have you prepared a master schedule?
9. Have you prepared a production schedule?

Chapter 7

Finding Original Ideas

Why should the advertiser seek original ideas? Surely, academics might argue, you need merely list the advantages of your product or service, and prospects will decide whether or not to buy.

However, those who earn a living from selling will know that business is not like that. To start with, you cannot instruct people to read your advertisements: you must catch their attention; then, in competition with surrounding type matter and pictures, entice reluctant, busy eyes to scan your message and decide to read on. If, after that, the reader is disturbed by telephones ringing, queries from colleagues, questions from husbands or wives, noisy children or the neighbours' radio, he or she must be sufficiently interested in your advertisement to make a point of returning to it.

But that is just the start. Having read your message, prospects must be so convinced by the arguments that desire in some form is aroused and a specific course of action is taken in your favour. Such action may be as non-committal as thinking sufficiently well of your brand to accept it when offered, or as positive as sending a coupon and cheque immediately.

A list of selling points is unlikely even to catch the reader's notice, let alone develop his or her interest so intensely that your copy is read. But if the list is given an amusing or unusual headline, which in turn is supported by a compelling picture, the chances of it being scanned are much improved. If the list is then introduced in an interesting way as part of a selling theme, and the reader is told clearly and simply what action to take, we have the elements of a logical sales message. But even then there is an enormous difference between a cold, deliberate presentation and one which has all the humour, soul or drama of an effective advertisement.

Let us return to the salesman. Before attempting to sell an expensive product or service he will try to establish a feeling of mutual understanding and respect with his customer. From such empathy will spring trust, and thence a basis for serious discussion which may eventually lead to a sale. Failure to build this important bridge will much reduce the salesman's chances of success.

Again, if the salesman is clean and smartly dressed and presents himself well, confidence is created, whereas flashy clothes and a tendency to bluster may undermine credibility.

These elementary principles of salesmanship apply equally to your advertisement, although a study of almost any newspaper or magazine will show that advertisers do not always understand their importance. A badly presented advertisement equates with a salesman in a cheap, ill-fitting suit and rumpled shirt, while extravagant claims, similar in many respects to the failings of an overdressed representative, may nullify an otherwise sound proposition.

Organise the main selling theme

From the observations in this chapter so far it is clear that an advertisement works better when the arguments are introduced in a novel, interesting and convincing way. But finding original or unusual ideas that attract and then persuade is not easy. The task will be simplified, however, if you adopt the following techniques:

1. List the advantages to the customer

Because you are so familiar with your product or service it is possible to overlook features which would benefit or attract the customer and provide a platform for a powerful advertisement. For example, a taxi firm which also runs a minibus on regular journeys for commercial customers might have seats available for private individuals or be able to offer the empty vehicle for hire at very special rates on return trips. Likewise, a builder might have special experience and skills, say, in repairing slate roofs or working with stone. In both of these cases, although there are interesting stories to be told and deals to explain, the proprietors may overlook the importance of what, to them, are everyday matters.

When preparing a written list of benefits to the customer it is important, therefore, to include *everything* you can offer, and devote some thought to the advantages derived from them. Define every point as simply as you can so that even a person unconnected with your trade or industry would understand the description. Of course this may not be possible in the case of highly technical subjects, but do avoid jargon where you can. For instance, 'the latest electronics systems in aircraft' might be better than 'state-of-the-art avionics', or 'transport' is better than 'physical distribution'. Simplicity, as you will see, adds punch and impetus to your advertising; how sensible, then, to enrol its advantages for yourself when taking the very first step towards finding good ideas. Simple thoughts are unlikely to stem from a complex analysis.

2. Consider the benefits or motives which encourage action
Having compiled the list, put it to one side for further thought later the same day or, better still, the day after. A fresh mind finds new angles, new advantages, new ideas. Now ask yourself:

> If I were a prospective customer, why would I use this product or service?
> What would there be in it for me?
> Why should I change my present method, or brand, or supplier?
> What would persuade me to buy it? Price? Quality? Convenience? Reliability?

Always examine your offer from the customer's viewpoint. His or her needs and preferences are of prime consequence. Research, albeit in an elementary form, may help greatly by revealing unsuspected facts and attitudes.

3. Consider the market
Next you should consider your product or service in relation to both the conventional markets and any peripheral fields. Although much of this work will have been done when planning the campaign, you may now, from your analysis of benefits to the customer and buying motives, have discovered additional possibilities. The markets and your place in them will determine the level of sophistication required, the importance of price, the need to influence stockists, the length of your message and many other factors.

This process of placing your thoughts on logical routes and rejecting unsuitable pathways will quickly lead you towards writing simple statements which, although probably uninspired at this stage, will at least provide a tangible beginning from which ideas will eventually spring.

Getting attention: 1

For a practical example we can return to Mr XYZ — the art materials retailer mentioned in Chapter 1 — to see how he approaches his problems. You will recall that he has recently been appointed the area agent for a new instant lettering system. To support an intensive direct mail programme he has booked 20cm × 2-column spaces in the local newspaper and a quarter-page series in the monthly newsletter published by the town's chamber of commerce. First he lists the advantages of the new system and the benefits of buying from his business:

Benefits of new instant lettering system

(a) Sheets cost slightly less than other transfer systems of comparable size and quality.
(b) Characters are formed from a new, stronger material which is less likely to crack or disintegrate during transfer.
(c) Carefully selected range of typefaces includes all the most widely used styles plus 20 new, exclusive faces.
(d) Wide range of ornaments, rules and accessories.
(e) Excellent selection of jumbo characters for display purposes, in many sizes and ten different colours.
(f) Catalogue supplied free to bona fide businesses and artists.
(g) When given specimen sheets to test, the directors of a local art studio were enthusiastic about several of the features, especially the ease of transfer and range of faces.

Benefits of buying from XYZ store

(a) Complete range of 'Instantype' sheets always in stock, with double or treble supplies of the most popular faces.
(b) If large quantities of certain faces needed, supplies can be posted immediately from the factory direct to customers.
(c) Thirty-day settlement terms for approved commercial customers. Generous scale of discounts allowed on all art materials and equipment supplied each month.
(d) A new delivery service will be offered to regular customers within about 15 miles. Orders received by 10 am delivered same day.
(e) Comprehensive range of art and drawing materials, accessories and equipment. Special items supplied to order.
(f) Catalogues, data sheets and supplementary lists will be presented in a free binder to business customers. Additions and revisions automatically sent when necessary.

Two stationers in his town carry limited stocks of art materials but cater mainly for amateurs. One of these competitors sells a range of instant lettering sheets which are unsuitable for professional artists, studios or drawing offices. The nearest important competitor, in a town some ten miles away, has a delivery service and until now has dominated the local market. Research indicates, however, that inefficiency and complacency have led to severe criticism by many customers. It seems probable that a new supplier will be welcome, but prospects must first be convinced that the lettering system is satisfactory. Outstanding buying motives will be the range of styles available, and quick, dependable deliveries.

With these facts in mind, the retailer can now write four elementary statements which sum up the deal he is offering:

(a) 'Instantype' is a new lettering system that is easier to use, comes in a wide selection of faces: all the practical, everyday styles, plus 20 new and exclusive designs.
(b) As well as 'Instantype' we stock an extensive range of art materials, accessories and equipment for studios, business people, drawing offices, professional artists and amateurs.
(c) Our service to important clients will include fast, reliable deliveries, and we shall ensure that customers are kept in touch with new products, new ideas, the latest techniques and type styles.
(d) Our prices are keen, terms of business competitive.

From these sentences spring two simple truths: the range of products — especially the lettering system — he sells and the service he will offer cannot be beaten locally. These specific and basic ideas must be explained to every important prospect within 15 miles, and in no circumstances can he allow such fundamental facts to be hidden among a confusing mass of extra claims.

The retailer now clearly understands what he must convey, but finding a new, unusual and memorable way of saying it will need further work, since inspiration is unlikely to arrive by magic. Pen in hand is usually more effective than head in hand.

He writes, 'The range of products I sell and the service I offer cannot be beaten locally.' The strongest word in that sentence is 'beaten'. Perhaps it could be used in a slogan or catch-line, or perhaps the word 'unmatchable' would lead his thoughts somewhere.

He tries to simplify his reasoning and then realises that the main purpose of his advertising is to launch the new instant lettering which has 20 exclusive typefaces. Perhaps a series of advertisements could illustrate the best of these styles under the headline 'You'll never match this'. Then a bold sign-off to the text describing his service could read 'and you'll never match that'.

Now he must decide whether the idea can be echoed in the mailing scheme, and he will therefore prepare draft letters and literature to satisfy himself that a complete campaign can be founded on this approach. In the next chapter we shall see how he writes the advertisement copy, and we shall return to the theme once more in Chapter 15 which deals with direct mail.

Note that the retailer has rejected the temptation to find a clever idea or slogan that has no logical connection with his marketing problem. The solution has emerged from a methodical assessment of the benefits he can offer prospects, their buying motives and, in this particular case, the weaknesses of a competitor.

Of course the process of finding original ideas is both difficult to define and debatable. The number of solutions to every problem is infinite; there is never a 'best' answer, although with experience to guide us we can usually say whether or not a certain approach is likely to succeed. There are no infallible guidelines, but the rules of advertising which you will find in the next chapter are worth observing, and particularly the need to be simple, direct and positive.

Getting attention: 2

Let us now examine a second example and return to the problems encountered by the partners mentioned in Chapter 1 who produce chairs, stools and settees of excellent quality in a variety of designs: their main distributors are a number of London stores, but having moved to larger premises the partners now wish to expand by supplying new, smaller stores within 50 miles of the factory. Most of these potential stockists are willing to accept the furniture on a trial basis provided the lines are backed by some form of advertising.

After investigating the cost of advertisement space in suitable local magazines and newspapers, and having allocated a generous sum for production costs, the partners believe a test campaign is justified. Now they are looking for an original and distinctive theme. First they list the main advantages, including the manufacturing methods which in this case are of special interest to buyers:

(a) *Types of furniture*
Dining chairs, including carvers, in two designs.
Easy chairs and settees in three designs.
Stools in kitchen, bar and garden designs.

(b) *Materials*
Finest yews, oaks and mahoganies, or other timbers to order, all properly seasoned. Timbers and veneers carefully selected and matched.
Upholstery in finest leathers or handwoven fabrics.

(c) *Designs*
By leading industrial designers.

(d) *Manufacture*
After machining, every component is examined and finished as necessary by hand before assembly. Every piece is then inspected before being waxed or polished by specialists using traditional methods.

Upholstery is by craftsmen, again using traditional methods and materials.
Every piece is critically inspected and approved by one of the partners before despatch.
In no way can the manufacturing processes be described as mass production.

(e) *Guarantee*
Apart from reasonable wear, accidental damage or deliberate abuse, every piece of furniture is guaranteed for five years. To maintain a reputation for exceptional quality, this guarantee is always honoured generously.

From these points it is apparent that the partners are producing a range of products with special attributes: a compromise between pieces which are made completely by hand, and the mass produced furniture to be seen in stores throughout the UK.

There is no need to seek or devise a very special selling point since the main reason for buying the furniture is inherent in the materials and production methods. Everyone admires craftsmanship. Most people will be happy to buy such furniture if they can afford it, and the majority of owners would be flattered by the applause and compliments of friends and family.

The pieces satisfy this need that many men and women feel for prestige and the envy of others. The partners understand that principle very well and therefore believe their advertisements must emphasise the exclusive designs they offer. Now an original idea must be found that explains all this in an interesting and attractive way. The first action is to write four elementary statements:

(a) We make dining chairs, easy chairs, settees and stools in fine materials.
(b) Styles are by leading designers.
(c) Modern equipment, craftsmanship and individual finishing are combined at every stage to produce furniture of manifest distinction.
(d) Buyers may select pieces from retailer's stock; or we will quote for and make to order special combinations of timbers and upholstery in any of the standard designs.

From this summary it is clear that the most important benefits offered are quality, design and choice, which eventually lead the partners to the phrase 'As you like it'. This can be adapted to 'Furniture as you like it' or 'Leather as you like it' or, indeed, in many other ways. The idea seems to have good possibilities, which will be tested when they write the copy for their advertisements in the campaign to come. In the next chapter we shall see how they fare.

To inexperienced advertisers the techniques recommended here probably seem unnecessary. Why, for example, take the trouble to list benefits and special features which you have known about and appreciated for years? Why write a few elementary paragraphs summarising them? The answer is contained in the first question: familiarity and a thorough knowledge of a product or service tend to hide or camouflage the fundamental advantages that prospects may need. Moreover, every good advertisement conveys its proposition in a way that is quickly and easily understood. You cannot expect readers or audiences to make a special effort to interpret your message, and a simple story is therefore vital.

For those who offer a product or service and know its every feature, this process of simplification can be extremely difficult. Further, the very act of writing about the various benefits and the buying motives of potential customers often helps you find and develop ideas.

Strangely, an independent adviser, such as an advertising agent, will usually recognise very quickly the most valuable attributes of a product and analyse them with greater ease. Nevertheless, for those who conduct their own advertising the task is not impossible and is an essential prelude to effective copywriting.

Checklist

1. Have you listed every feature and advantage of your product or service?
2. What's in it for the customer?
3. Why does he or she need it, and why buy it?
4. Have you considered the market and your place in it?
5. Have you written a few simple statements to outline the deal you are offering?
6. Have you studied these statements and sought powerful words or phrases which express the very heart of your proposition?
7. Are there any subsidiary benefits which dilute your arguments and can be abandoned?

Chapter 8

Writing Effective Copy

The process of preparing a summary of product benefits and related notes described in the last chapter will again be valuable when writing the text or 'copy' for advertisements. Previously our efforts were directed to finding original ideas and themes, which are primarily a means of gaining attention. Now we are concerned with arousing and maintaining the reader's interest while we explain our proposition and create desire for the product, or influence his attitude towards it. He must then be told precisely what action to take and be encouraged to take it.

First, as an introduction to the subject, you will learn much from examining advertisements in any newspaper or magazine and selecting those which you believe may achieve these basic objectives. Do the headlines and illustrations encourage you to read on? Do you fully understand the text? Is it exciting or just plain boring? Is there the slightest chance of your wanting to take action of some kind in favour of the advertiser? Do you know exactly what he wants you to do?

Remember, you are deliberately studying the advertisement, whereas under normal circumstances a reader has no such duty and must therefore be enticed and persuaded. Viewed in this way, the copywriter's task is formidable. Luckily there are rules which help to solve many of the problems, but the writer will still profit from dedication and common sense. An interest in and understanding of matters which stimulate the emotions and desires, with particular heed to such factors as age, social class and sex, will also be valuable.

The rules of advertising

The first guide-lines are provided by 15 rules which I believe to be essential to success in all forms of advertising. Although they encompass many of the principles explained elsewhere in this book, they are of such importance that I make no apologies for repeating them.

1. *Be simple*
   Never let your reasoning or your approach be clouded by complex thoughts. Simplify and refine. Where possible, use everyday words in short easy sentences that everyone can grasp. Eliminate technical jargon where feasible.

2. *Be interesting*
   Try to be exciting and enthusiastic. If you can arouse curiosity so much the better. Avoid a long and tedious list of extravagant claims. Readers are not interested in your products as such, but only in the benefits to be derived from them.

3. *Be direct*
   Come to the point quickly. Be frugal with sentences. Sometimes you can even cut out the first one completely. Then cut unnecessary words, especially adjectives, if you can. Explain your proposition economically, but never sacrifice words that are needed for style or rhythm.

4. *Be positive*
   Negative statements are usually best converted to positive encouragement. For example, 'Don't miss this special offer' is weaker than 'Special offer. Order today!' Avoid negative exhortations such as 'Why not visit our showrooms.' Find a positive substitute: 'See them in our showrooms NOW!'

5. *Be sensible*
   Tortuous reasoning can so easily get out of hand, becoming completely illogical. Ask yourself whether a man or woman of average intelligence would be likely to believe your assertions or even appreciate the point you are trying to make.

6. *Be factual*
   If readers wish to explore the world of imaginative writing they will turn to suitable literature. By all means garnish your arguments, though sparingly, when style or the need for a colourful presentation make it necessary, but do complete the story as quickly as you can.

7. *Be brief*
   How often have you skipped an advertisement because it looked difficult to read? Small areas of type invite the eye because they are easily scanned.

   Unless you are confident that your brilliant prose will hold the reader enthralled, say what you must as briefly as you can. Then cut, and cut again.

8. *Be truthful and decent*
Every advertisement is checked by the publishers or contractors to ensure it complies with a code of practice laid down by the Advertising Standards Authority. Doubtful, extravagant or misleading claims, indecent illustrations or copy, and similar crimes against humanity, are reported to the ASA who will reject the advertisement if it breaks the rules.
Quite apart from these safeguards, however, it is most unwise to advertise dishonestly or attempt to gain attention through illustrations that titillate. Untruthful claims are soon disproved, and therefore you are most unlikely to gain repeat orders. Sexually stimulating pictures, sometimes with crude headlines, are occasionally seen in trade journals, but readers may justifiably suspect that the service or product in question has so few attractions that the advertisement is a last resort.

9. *Be different and original*
Within rational limits, your message will win impact and interest if it is presented from an original angle or in an unusual way. Headlines, illustrations, text and slogans, or even the shapes of advertisements can be used for this purpose. Do not, however, overstep the border between an exciting idea and the ridiculous or downright silly. Every member of your audience must be able to understand at once the point you are making. Humour is an excellent tool but it must be directly relevant to the notion you want to impart.
By studying current press advertisements and radio and television commercials you will come to appreciate the danger of being too clever. National advertisers are sometimes the worst offenders.

10. *Repeat important selling points*
The purpose of an advertisement is usually to convey the most important ideas or points which will help to sell the product or service. Selecting these essentials, finding a good theme and then writing the copy require very considerable effort by the advertiser. Having finished the job, he or she will read it through several times and conclude that even a simpleton can grasp the tale. After so much labour it is difficult to admit that yours is just another ad.

Sadly, you can never be sure that prospects will read your entire message, and when they do you cannot expect them to remember every point you make. In most cases they will just skim through the copy before their attention is caught by other items on the page or they turn over.

During that brief flirtation with your advertisement every element in it must highlight and strengthen the main ideas you want to transmit. By reducing the number of points and repeating, emphasising and illustrating them so that they are perceived and remembered, the copy becomes very much more effective. Of course, the points can be repeated in different ways, using different words, to hold the reader's interest.

Experience has proved the great value of repetition. Vary the setting by all means, but success stems from constant reminders. Of course there is always the danger of becoming a bore, and this explains the value of humour. Readers and viewers seldom tire of the same old joke if it is clever and well presented. Note, however, that the bizarre may offend.

11. *Seek and hold attention*

Throughout this book there is reference to 'interest' and 'attention', without which every advertisement will fail. But in truth the problem is not as elementary as it seems. Anyone, for example, can gain a child's attention by making a loud noise, but this will not automatically channel his interest towards an object. Much better to tap the object in order to attract his interest so that eyes and ears are co-ordinated.

In advertising, the same principle obtains. There must be a logical and simple link between the means of seeking attention and converting it into interest. This fundamental rule is overlooked far too often.

The headline 'Be a millionaire' is certain to catch attention, but if it is tied to a new way of saving money on fuel the concept is ludicrous. The same headline, however, is obviously acceptable in an advertisement for football pools.

The process of holding attention so that the prospect reads all or most of your message depends on the information you impart, the words you use, the length of your text and whether it looks easy to read. The eye automatically rejects a grey mass of words unrelieved by paragraphs. Conversely, it is attracted by small areas of words broken down into short paragraphs. Subheadings set in bold type induce the eye to read on. The mind is stimulated by unusual or exciting statements and will need to satisfy the curiosity they arouse.

Attention is held by offering the reader a series of positive benefits supported, if possible, by interesting illustrations. Words and phrases that create mental pictures are especially valuable. Reject 'comfortable house' in favour of 'cosy home' or replace 'mothers' with 'mums', because the images these words evoke are so much more vivid and friendly.

Never talk down to your prospects; never allow your claims to sound pompous. Disbelief and alienation destroy attention immediately.

12. *Tell the reader what he or she must do*

One of the greatest problems encountered by those who sell direct is deciding when and how to close a sale. Usually it is the most delicate part of the whole process of selling, since the customer reaches a point where he or she must reject the proposition outright, delay a decision or actually buy.

Mail order advertisements face exactly the same problems but lack the advantages of face-to-face selling where a customer's objections can be countered with reasoned arguments. The exhortation to buy must therefore be expressed strongly and clearly, with powerful encouragement to act at once. There may even be a tangible incentive, such as a discount for ordering by a certain date.

Quite apart from lucid instructions in the copy on why and how to order, the reader must be further persuaded through bold display lines or ornaments pointing into a coupon or order form, backed by even stronger encouragement on the coupon or form itself. Say it plainly, say it urgently, say it vigorously, say it often.

In fact every advertisement should tell the readers exactly what you want them to do. Just as salespeople try to close a deal, advertisers should give specific and positive guidance with such phrases as 'Write or ring today for details' or 'Ring 123 4567 NOW!' or 'Post the coupon NOW — no stamp needed.'

Even if the intention of your advertisement is to seek the consumers' acceptance of your product in the shops, always tell them where they can buy it, with an explicit exhortation such as 'From your newsagent NOW!' Note, too, that suggestion is an extremely potent incitement to action.

13. *Test the medium*
The usefulness or pulling power of the medium in which an advertisement is published must be assessed as accurately as possible before long-term orders are placed.

14. *Test the copywriting and design*
Assessing the effectiveness of what you say, how you say it and how you present it is of great consequence to every advertiser, and of crucial importance to the small business with a modest publicity budget.
Copy and media testing are discussed in Chapter 10.

15. *Avoid direct comparisons with competitors by name*
From time to time a large national advertiser and his advertising agent are blessed with a breath-taking and audacious idea. 'Let's slam our competitors,' they exclaim, 'and what's more, let's attack the blighters by name.' Marketing specialists everywhere gasp at such courage and originality. Taken aback by the sheer genius of this strategy, business journals salute the perpetrators — whereupon smaller companies follow the lead so widely applauded.
To appraise the wisdom of such direct comparisons one has only to imagine dealing with a salesman who insists on naming and criticising his competitors. Most people would ask themselves why he is so worried about other products, and whether in fact he is offering something inferior. Sensibly, they then investigate competing brands and may in consequence buy elsewhere.
Exactly the same reactions can be expected from an advertisement but the advertiser is in a much weaker position since he cannot answer the questions arising from the reader's uncertainties.
Of course there is no harm in an advertiser claiming that he sells the very best available; he can even compare, in general terms, certain features of his product or service with others on the market and claim advantages. But the moment he names competitors his arguments become weaker. Furthermore, he is actually drawing attention to rivals and giving them free publicity. Those of sound mind may conclude that this is indeed a perilous path.
Note, too, that logic and hard facts do not always persuade prospects to buy. Appearance, colour, prestige, trust, habit, emotional appeal and a host of other intangibles will often influence a transaction.

These easy rules are overlooked by far too many advertisers. Most errors arise from self-inflicted confusion, which commonly originates from a failure to analyse basic problems, find elementary solutions and express ideas in everyday language whenever possible.

Style

When the pen is interposed between brain and paper, even the most eloquent people tend to use inelegant words and phrases. Likewise, formality and a strange, awkward style result from most attempts at copywriting by those unversed in the art. So, having written a first paragraph, ask yourself whether you would be likely to use those exact words in that very same way in conversation. Then repeat the process until the work is complete.

Informality and a friendly approach are essential in writing the copy for almost every kind of advertisement. Nowadays, even the more conservative institutions, such as banks and insurance companies, have found that it pays to present themselves as warm and caring.

If you have difficulty in finding a suitable idiom, simply cast your pen aside and imagine how you might explain your proposition or describe your product to a friend. Then write those very words down immediately, overlooking style or grammar. Now try to refine the statements so that even a person of low intelligence would understand your meaning exactly. Then edit and polish by cutting unnecessary words or phrases and trying to create a pleasing rhythm. This will come more comfortably from short, pithy expressions and by using words of Anglo-Saxon origin wherever you can.

Words such as 'free', 'now' or 'save' — however trite — retain their power, appeal and value. Do not confuse them with descriptive clichés or tired phrases, which are best avoided because they are weak from overwork. Good substitutes can usually be found.

Contrast in pace, acquired by varying the length of sentences and paragraphs and selecting suitable words, can be used to spotlight important points and to hold the reader's attention.

Emphasis can also be achieved by placing words or phrases of major consequence at the end of a sentence or paragraph. To maintain an unbroken flow of interest, each sentence or paragraph should be connected with the previous one wherever possible. You should therefore devote much thought to the structure of your copy.

Aim, too, at an elegant, balanced arrangement of words, phrases, sentences and paragraphs which conveys elementary ideas and strong mental pictures in such a way, and in such a sequence, that the reader is encouraged to absorb your entire message. A sharp break in the story may result in immediate loss of interest.

Remember, your own achievements are unlikely to impress or excite the prospect, whose chief concern will be the benefits he or his family or his business will reap from the product or service you are advertising. So mention your firm only when the facts suggest advantages, such as special expertise or reliability, from which the reader will have something to gain.

Motivation and appeal

Advertising agents make a detailed and continuous study of the motives which encourage people of all ages to buy or react in certain ways. With a little thought we can easily list the more obvious objectives and desires that everyone has, such as the search for security and safety, the need for acclaim, sexual ambitions and family or team loyalties. Many, perhaps all, of these motives spring from natural instincts, which can be aroused by basic stimuli.

The subject is extremely complex and one which we cannot even begin to investigate or summarise in a general book of this kind. Nevertheless, it is important to know that many transactions are influenced by innate wants and desires, and to acknowledge that an appeal to such inborn needs will in many cases be more successful than a cold and logical presentation of benefits.

For example, an advertisement for new homes might illustrate them under the headline 'From only £XXX freehold'. But if an attractive line drawing of a man and wife holding hands were added to the picture and the headline were changed to 'Happy families from just £XX weekly', the proposition would be transformed, becoming not only an appeal to natural instincts but also explaining how easily the desires so aroused can be satisfied.

Manifestly, every advertiser should think deeply about the motives which will persuade prospects to buy the wares or services he offers. Sometimes the main instincts or emotions will be apparent, but in other cases they may be obscure. For example, although an industrial buyer may be influenced largely by the performance and price of a component, he also has normal susceptibilities and may respond to an appeal to certain emotions if the approach is sufficiently subtle and in good taste. Thus a close-up illustration of a man winking, with the headline, 'Even the Chairman applauded when we changed to ZX systems', would suggest much improved results, leading to praise by business superiors. Thus, by indirectly seeking an emotional response and adding a touch of humour, the copywriter strengthens the approach and brings a little sparkle to what otherwise might be a dull advertisement.

Note, incidentally, the use of a capital 'C' in 'Chairman' to emphasise the suggestion of 'high places'.

In future you will, I hope, study advertisements in the national and local newspapers, magazines and trade journals to appraise the copywriters' skills, learn from the best and perhaps criticise others.

Slogans

A good slogan provides a connecting link between advertisements in every medium you use, and can be reiterated in literature, displays, van designs and the like to remind customers or prospects time and again of an important benefit to be gained from your product or service. Properly used, it will eventually create a valuable association of ideas.

To find a slogan, you should first define its purpose and then search for memorable, pithy phrases which summarise graphically, in a few words, the deal you offer. Of course this demands much time and work, and you must be completely happy with the result before using it. Application is more likely to find the right answer than inspiration. Decide exactly what you want to say and then hunt for just the right words. Rhythm and alliteration often help.

Examples

Now we can return to our enterprising supplier of art materials, who in the previous chapter had decided that the headline, 'You'll never match this', accompanied by a bold sign-off, 'And you'll never match that', might be used in his press advertising. Now he will write the copy to see whether the concept can be developed sensibly.

Having already listed the advantages of the new lettering system and of buying from the XYZ store, he can start writing at once:

First draft

Headline: ***You'll never match this . . .**

It's the all-new *Instantype* system of transfer lettering. Stronger, easier to use, but costs less. It comes in all the popular faces plus 20 exclusive styles. At XYZ we stock the complete range — just another reason why so many professional artists, studios and businesses come to us for their art materials, accessories and equipment.

*This new, graceful type-style is called 'Romantica': available in sizes 8pt to 96pt and exclusive to *Instantype*.

Panel: **Instantype book**
Comes free to professional and business users.
Ring today for details.

Subhead: **XYZ service**
To regular business customers we deliver daily; phone orders received before 10am guaranteed to arrive by 3pm! Generous discount scale on monthly accounts. Big range of art and drawing materials, accessories, equipment always in stock. Special items supplied to order.

Catch-line: **. . . and you'll never match that!**

So ring us today for a preliminary chat. As a starter we'll be glad to deliver the *Instantype* book plus the XYZ catalogue — all free and without obligation.

XYZ ART SUPPLIES (plus logotype)
Address and telephone number

This first attempt outlines his basic offer quite well, but would it win more interest and work more effectively if a friendlier style were introduced? This series of advertisements is intended to support a direct mail campaign, which is essentially a person-to-person medium, well suited to an informal approach. The proprietor also recalls that before deciding to carry 'Instantype' he gave several sheets to a studio for testing and that the subsequent report was enthusiastic. The copy is therefore revised as follows:

Second draft

Headline: **You'll never match this**

Before stocking the all-new *Instantype* system of transfer lettering, we asked professional artists to test it. 'You'll never match this for value,' they said. 'It's stronger, easier to use, but costs less.'

Surprised they were, too, to find it comes in all the popular faces plus 20 exclusive styles unmatchable elsewhere. Our headline, for instance, is set in 'Romantica', available in 8pt to 96pt sizes. You'll see this and the rest of the range in the *Instantype* book supplied free to businesses.

Catch-line: **. . . and you'll never match this service**

To regular business customers we deliver daily. Ring before 10am for delivery by 3pm, guaranteed.

What's more, we carry a really big range of art and drawing materials, accessories and equipment. Generous discounts for monthly accounts. Special items supplied to order.

So ring today for your personal copies of the *Instantype* book and the XYZ catalogue. Phone before 10am, they'll be with you by 3: free and without obligation!

XYZ ART SUPPLIES (plus logotype)
Address and telephone number.

This revised draft seems to comply with the elementary rules of advertising. It is simple, interesting, direct, positive, sensible, factual, brief, decent and is likely to catch prospects' attention. The reader is told exactly what to do and the two most important items — 'Instantype' and the delivery service — are emphasised by repetition. Tests will eventually establish the advertisement's ability to pull enquiries. Much will depend on how the copy is presented, a subject discussed at length in the next chapter.

Meanwhile, let us examine the copywriting techniques used by the partners who manufacture chairs, settees and stools. You will recall that a press campaign is being planned to encourage new stockists, and that by analysing the various benefits to prospective buyers the partners have arrived at a headline or slogan, 'Furniture as you like it'. A first draft is attempted, and for convenience I will refer to the brand name as 'ABC'.

ABC (logotype)

Furniture as you like it

Dining and easy chairs
Settees
Stools

In oak, mahogany, yew. Or to order, in a timber of your choice. All seasoned well.

Upholstered in leathers, expertly selected; or fabrics handwoven with care.

Styles created by designers of eminence.

Every piece hand finished; traditionally polished.

Work closely overseen to safeguard our good repute.

To be admired at these establishments who will deliver from their stores, or will be greatly pleased to accept your order for work in the materials you choose.

List of stockists

ABC FURNITURE (logotype)

Just as you like it

Address line

The success of this distinctive approach will depend very much on the artist's presentation and especially the illustrations. Note that the careful selection of words and the rhythm in their arrangement are intended to create an atmosphere that suggests craftsmanship, without once using that jaded word. The big selling point, choice, is accentuated by repetition. Note, too, that in this example the rules of English grammar have been abandoned. Selling is the first priority, and while experienced copywriters usually prefer to comply with academic principles wherever possible, commercial needs are always paramount.

Apart from minor alterations to meet the artist's special wants or ideas, this first draft seems to be satisfactory.

Before we leave the subject of copywriting there are two further points to remember. First, if you are responsible for writing advertisement copy, never allow your efforts to be partly rewritten by colleagues. A 'committee' effort loses its impact and style, and may even become unintelligible. Of course you must show it to others and invite their comments if necessary. The facts must be correct; the prose should be easy to read and understand; the theme must be sensible. But always insist that you, the originator, have full control of the work within these bounds.

Second, you may be wondering how a writer estimates the number of words that will fit into a given space. An artist or designer can calculate such requirements with considerable accuracy, but at copywriting stage an approximate number is quite adequate. You need merely prepare a rough sketch of your advertisement, allocating a reasonable amount of space for headlines, other display type and illustrations. The remaining area, apart from margins, will be available for the text matter, or 'body copy' as it is usually known.

Now you allow about 20 words to the square inch (say 6 square centimetres) in 10 point type, or 30 words in 8 point, which is the smallest size that can be read comfortably. At design stage your artist may ask you to add or cut a few words, but for writing purposes these guide-lines are dependable unless you are using a series of long technical words.

Further information on the use of type is given in the next chapter.

Checklist

1. Have you referred to your list of benefits to the customer?
2. After writing your first draft, did you check that it complies with the rules of advertising?
3. Have you considered the prospects' buying motives?
4. Is the copy easy to read and friendly?
5. Will it fit the available space?

Chapter 9

Producing Eye-catching Advertisements

Having written the copy for your advertisement, you are now reaching what many people would regard as the most exciting and interesting stage: presenting the message in such a way that the idea will be immediately grasped by the casual reader, whose imagination and curiosity must be stimulated so strongly that he or she will want to read on.

During the process of finding an underlying theme and writing the copy, you will almost certainly have considered the kind of illustration needed, if any, to strengthen your signal to those you must influence.

Decide on the kind of illustration needed

Sometimes a picture can be used as a prime means of gaining attention. It may, for example, be unusual, humorous or have a direct appeal to, say, teenagers. If the style, design or appearance of a product is important there will be a good argument for making a picture of it the main component of an advertisement, simply because it is of outstanding significance to the prospect.

Sometimes a picture will have more than one purpose. For instance, showing mum, dad and the children in a saloon car depicts the family in happy, ideal circumstances, and at the same time illustrates the car itself. A photograph of a sports model occupied by a handsome young couple suggests adventures which many readers may wish to emulate. Compare these settings with the severe, often drab, pictures seen in so many of today's car advertisements and you may wonder whether a pinch of imagination and a little flair might be worth more than the volumes of impersonal research which may be responsible for this lack of inspiration.

As a general guide, you should use illustrations to compel the right kind of notice, supply information or add drama or excitement to your copy. But do remember that pictures are not obligatory and can sometimes be an expensive barrier to understanding.

Let us consider the case of an electronics instrument, made in a variety of versions by a number of companies. Apart from minor design differences, each version is virtually identical in appearance: a metal cabinet with a dial and three switches. The instrument's external designs are of absolutely no importance to prospective buyers, who are interested only in accuracy, reliability, price, and special features, if any, that would make a particular model more versatile. Thus there is no logical reason for illustrating the instrument, and using valuable space to do so is actually denying the reader additional information which might persuade him to send for a data sheet. On the other hand, a graph which showed at a glance certain performance advantages would be fully justified.

On occasions, a picture which is apparently unconnected with a product or service can be used to draw attention to an otherwise very dull subject. There must, however, be a sensible and clear link which can be explained and understood in a word or two.

Take as an example the DIY retailer mentioned in Chapter 2. During his search for job lots he has found a huge quantity of iron nails in different shapes and sizes. He can sell them at about half usual price, but must generate attention in an especially powerful way to counter the lack of interest in such mundane articles. First he must bring the deal to the notice of readers and then suggest that even if they have no present need for nails they will certainly want them soon, when they may have to pay the full price.

After discussing the presentation with his artist, the retailer agrees that a photograph shall be commissioned showing him and his staff peeping over a stack of crates which are more than shoulder high. The headline to the advertisement will read, 'To do you a favour we're up to our ears in them'. Body copy will then begin, 'Up to our ears in NAILS. Nails in every shape and size; all at half price or less . . .'

This combination of unusual illustration and 'teaser' headline is bound to be read, if only to satisfy enquiring minds.

Select the typeface

After reaching a provisional decision on the use of an illustration, it will be wise to devote some thought to the typefaces to be employed in your advertisement. Nowadays the subject is complicated by the great selection of styles available from photosetting processes and transfer lettering systems. In general, however, you should understand that there are four major classifications:

1. Typefaces suitable for body copy because they are easy to read when closely set and in small sizes.

2. Classical faces, developed mainly from the roman characters. In the smaller sizes they are sometimes used for body matter. In larger or bolder versions they are suitable for display if you wish to suggest prestige or formality.
3. Display faces, intended specifically for headlines, subheadings or where you want to emphasise a limited number of words. There is an enormous variety of these faces, which can be used to convey or suggest many different ideas or moods.
4. Decorative faces, which are so ornate that their use should always be restricted to just a very few words. Sometimes they are difficult to read even then.

Every one of these faces is identified by a name and many are available in different renderings of the basic style. Thus, for example, in the 'Garamond' range you can select from medium, medium italic, bold, bold italic, medium condensed, medium condensed italic, bold condensed and bold condensed italic. Sizes are based on the 'point' measurement system originally used for setting metal type. Most faces come in the scale 8 point to 72 point, but although 72 points are approximately 1 inch, it does not follow that a face in this size will be exactly 1 inch high, and in some cases it is much less.

From this very brief look at the subject of type selection you will appreciate that typography is best left to specialists, although you should be aware of the importance of using type to echo the mood of your message. You must always insist, however, that every word in your advertisement, whether it is display or text matter, is easy to read at a glance. Sadly, a number of the faces in the instant lettering systems are extremely difficult to translate and should be avoided.

Illustration techniques

Just as typefaces should be legible, your illustrations must always be easy to 'read' and therefore be sharp, with sufficient contrast to ensure that every detail is clearly distinguished. A flick through almost any magazine or newspaper will produce examples of 'muddy' pictures which are of no value whatsoever to the advertiser concerned. Yet with a little research and some guidance from your artist this pitfall is avoidable.

A survey of the publications to be used in your campaign will reveal the standard of reproduction in each. If pictures and type are indistinct in places and photographs are difficult to decipher, you must ensure your own illustrations are sharply defined by using only black and white, with no intermediate tones, and using typefaces that do not have fine serifs. If you must reproduce a photograph it should be retouched to reduce the number of tones, so that ideally you have just black, white, medium grey, light grey and dark grey.

Having established this simple rule, let us examine some of the illustration techniques commonly in use today:

1. *Line drawings*
   With these the artist works in black only on a white surface. This kind of illustration can be reversed photographically so that the lines appear in white on a black background. Type matter is easily mounted on such drawings and can also be reversed black to white if need be. Note, however, that very fine white lines may clog or even disappear completely, especially on coarse surfaces such as newsprint.
2. *Photographs*
   These enjoy the major advantage of suggesting realism or proof of an event or situation. Unfortunately a lot of people are amateur photographers and must be persuaded that only a professional can produce the picture standards so essential for advertisement illustration.

   Normally one would hesitate to retouch good photographs apart, perhaps, from a little cleaning up here and there. But when printing qualities are poor as, for example, in newspaper production, it may be essential to reduce the number of 'greys' accordingly, as previously described. Sometimes, too, a photograph of a product is out of date and will need appropriate retouching. The process demands a high degree of skill, however, and is therefore expensive. Often it will be cheaper to commission a new shot. In any case, do avoid very heavy retouching, which is immediately noticed by the reader, unless there is no alternative at a price you can afford. Your artist will usually have good advice to offer.

   Reproducing a photograph calls for a special half-tone technique since in commercial printing methods it is impossible to generate continuous tones. A screen is therefore interposed between the photograph and the film, from which a printing plate is eventually made so that the image is broken down into a series of dots. In the black areas the dots will virtually merge, while in white areas the dots will be extremely fine. Intermediate tones will be represented by heavy or light dots according to the strength of grey in the areas they represent.

Take a magnifying glass to any half-tone picture to grasp the principles of the process at once. You will see that coarse screens with much larger dots are used on rough surfaces, while on a smoother paper with a glossy finish the screen is much finer and has more dots to the square centimetre. The litho platemaker or process engraver grades his screens by numbers, or rasters, 25 being very coarse and 60 very fine.

3. *Line and tint or line and wash drawings*

   Sometimes an artist will produce a line drawing with areas of shade represented by a tint, which is simply a patch of dots or fine lines. He can lay the tint himself from instant lettering sheets or he may colour the tint area with blue pencil and ask the platemaker to lay the tint for him. The second method usually gives a cleaner result.

   Alternatively, he may lay a tone wash over the area to be shaded, and although in this case the printed result may be superior, the platemaker must produce a combined line and tone negative, which will be much more expensive.

4. *Scraper board drawings*

   Often based on original photographs, 'scrapers' and similar drawings are very largely used for newspaper advertisements. They have a crisp, interesting character which reproduces well on coarse surfaces. They are, however, expensive.

5. *Tone drawings*

   Air brush, wash, pencil or crayon drawings are sometimes used to create a specific atmosphere or decorative effect. Fashion artists, for example, often use wash or line-and-wash techniques.

6. *Mechanical and photographic effects*

   There are many methods of converting ordinary photographs into line illustrations with special qualities and features. Some cost very little but are extremely effective, while others may be beyond the budget of an average small business.

7. *Colour illustrations*

   Several of the techniques described so far can be incorporated in colour illustrations, but it is important to distinguish between simple combinations of colour and full colour printing.

   If, for example, you book an additional colour such as a standard red for your advertisement, it means that you can use that red for type matter, for rules, drawings or slabs of colour, or perhaps for a border. The form your artwork takes will differ little from black and white insertions except that the artist may separate the colours by means of a transparent sheet, called an overlay.

If, however, you have booked a space in full colour the illustration may consist of a colour photograph, colour transparency or a drawing in full colour. You may also reproduce lettering or decorative features in any colour you select. Of course, you should ensure that the standards of design and artwork are exceptionally high to justify the expenditure on a four-colour insertion,* and it would be a mistake to send a colour transparency to the publishers with a few words of copy, and ask them to produce an advertisement.

8. *Symbols and name styles*
Closely allied to illustration and design techniques are the subjects of house symbols and name styles, sometimes called 'logotypes'. The latter are simply metal 'slugs' or blocks used in letterpress printing to reproduce a device unobtainable in standard typefaces, and normally employed to add distinction or a means of recognition to a firm's stationery and publicity material. Nowadays the term is used in a generic sense to describe every kind of trade mark.

Many businesses introduce their own complete house styles by using common design elements in everything they publish, and on their packs, vans, displays and the like. Advice on such a project is not strictly within the scope of this volume. I would stress, however, that if you are contemplating the creation of a 'corporate image', do appoint a first-rate artist or studio and ensure that the design motifs are versatile, easily adaptable and unlikely to be affected by the demands of fashion in the years to come.

Finding the right artist

So far in this section we have assumed that you will originate the basic theme of your press advertisements and prepare the copy, although the work could, of course, be passed to a professional writer if you can afford this. But now we reach a stage where skilled help is essential and you must seek the services of either an art studio,

* Full colour printing is often called four-colour work because red, blue, yellow and black printing plates are needed for the process.

or a properly trained artist with long experience in preparing designs and artwork for every kind of advertising material. If he, or she, has worked for a bona fide advertising agency and consequently understands the purpose of your advertisements within the marketing plan, so much the better.

A young person with art school training and little understanding of the world of commerce will not be suitable. Similarly, a nephew's ability to draw Donald Duck should be properly admired but firmly rejected as a qualification for designing your ads.

An equally wrong decision would be to send your copy and pictures to the publisher. He will usually prepare your artwork at very low rates as an incentive to advertise in his publication, and the temptation to accept an offer which apparently saves you money is understandable. But if you want your advertising to succeed there is no sound alternative to engaging an independent professional or studio. The significance of that principle will become clearer as we work through this chapter, but first you may welcome the following guidance on how to select the right person.

Looking for the right type of studio

Artists run their businesses in many different ways. Some work from home, where the 'studio' may be just a table in a corner of a living room or a more elaborate affair with modern equipment, including perhaps a machine for enlarging or reducing photographically and supplying photoprints. Other artists prefer to work from a studio away from home. Some of these operate alone; some practise in a group, which may include a number of specialists such as illustrators, figure artists or typographers.

Although artists will often describe themselves as 'designers', this term can mislead; some may be unwilling or indeed unable to prepare finished artwork from which printing plates are made, while others much prefer to see the job through from layout to artwork and then may even supply suitable negatives or positives on film for the publishers.

Some studios are run by business men or women, who may employ a number of artists directly, or may just provide 'desk space' for self-employed artists who, in return, agree to work for them at a special low rate but are also free to accept commissions from elsewhere.

The ideal artist for those who run small businesses is probably one whose experience enables him to offer a complete service, in which sensible design allows artwork to be supplied at reasonable cost and ensures that the subsequent advertisements will reproduce well despite the technical problems presented by certain processes and the papers on which the publications are printed. If the artist balances a natural tendency to create good art within the restraints imposed by commercial need, and appreciates the marketing tactics you intend to employ, so much the better.

Such artists do exist although, of course, they are rare. A small studio may therefore be the best answer and may in fact give you certain advantages: specialists will add sparkle and distinction to designs and illustrations; repetitive work may be done by trainees at lower rates; modern equipment may improve the results but cost you less; team action will produce work very quickly in an emergency; artists benefit from studio discussions on new techniques and the like, so that output generally improves. Moreover, the representative who calls on you will be fully experienced in the hard world of business needs and will protect your interests when artists' ideas are too fanciful or impracticable.

To find an artist or studio that is right for you, the first step should be to ask business friends and suppliers for recommendations. Then, of course, you can consult local directories, chambers of commerce and similar bodies. Compose a list of names and ask the candidates to call.

The process of selection

Your first meeting will be extremely important. If the artist or representative is on time, is well dressed and tidy, and introduces himself confidently but in a manner that acknowledges your position as the client, you are off to a good start. If the caller is an artist a certain eccentricity may be forgiven, although long experience has taught me that those at the top of their profession are seldom scruffy or dirty.

During this interview you will be presented with specimens of work accompanied by a proud commentary on the demands of the clients involved and how they were met. Watch for variety of jobs, versatility, the standing of the clients served and the products they sell, the standard of design, illustration, reproduction and, equally telling, how much trouble has been taken to introduce the specimens to you in a sensible, clean and impressive way. Logically, you would not expect an artist to present your product or service effectively if he is incapable of doing just that for his own work.

I think at this early meeting it would be unwise to investigate costs. By asking how much 'this design' or 'that drawing' actually came to, you will be revealing an ignorance which can add nothing to your fund of information. Without background knowledge of the original brief or the source of reference for an illustration you cannot possibly judge whether a fee is extortionate or reasonable.

More important at this juncture will be the relationship you are likely to build with the artist or studio representative. This person you may see once a week or more for, perhaps, years to come. You may impart to him much confidential intelligence, discuss forthcoming ventures, and seek advice on how to present a new campaign, reduce costs to fit your budget or on whether an ad can be produced by tomorrow afternoon. Do you think his opinions will be sound? Is he a true professional? Is he enthusiastic and confident about the service he offers? Will he gain your respect? Are you likely to welcome his company or do you find his mannerisms or attitudes abrasive? Above all, do you trust him?

After interviewing all the candidates you will probably select two or three who merit further investigation, or there may be one who in your estimation is so outstanding that a decision will be almost automatic. But whatever the outcome, you are firmly advised to inspect their places of work and seek opinions from independent sources before placing orders. So make your appointment, and during the visit try to assess the volume of work in hand and the quality of the clients served. If there are several artists and you are invited to have a word with each, ask them about jobs in progress and the contribution they are making. An efficient team will be proud to explain how 'impossible' deadlines are welcomed and met.

If the artists are obviously very experienced and anxious to show you specimens of work, you will quickly sense their dedication. If the phone is busy and people are engaged in what appear to be urgent discussions you will again draw favourable conclusions.

In my experience, studios are rarely tidy, especially when busy: card, paper and similar materials must be cut to size in a hurry; typesetting and photoprints are spread around desks and tables; work in hand may be put to one side to dry or to await the arrival of photographs or other components. After a hectic day, a studio is always littered with off-cuts and overflowing waste bins. Do not be surprised, then, if you enter a strange place of apparent chaos and confusion from which designs, drawings and artwork emerge out of complete disarray.

During your visit enquire about and ask to see the equipment used. A well-built darkroom with modern photoprinting, a good copying machine and similar assets are virtually essential to cope with a regular flow of artwork. If you have selected a freelance artist it is perhaps even more important to visit his work-place and see the conditions for yourself. A genuine professional with a group of sound clients will earn a very comfortable living and so is in a position to rent or buy suitable premises. Do not expect the studio to be immaculate or even expensively furnished. But make sure it is functional, and if he or she has no photoprinting or copying equipment, ask about the source of supply, which may be nearby. If the room is shabby and there is scant evidence that he works for companies of some repute, or if excuses are made to prevent your visit, do investigate his claims very thoroughly.

Finally, before you place orders it is advisable to ask local printers of substance whether they know of the studio or artist. When you find one who does, ask for an assessment of the quality of work, technical understanding and reliability of the candidate. If the reply is critical, investigate further.

To the inexperienced, such a thorough exploration may seem unnecessary or at least excessive. Please believe me, it is not. On the perimeter of the advertising business one finds a number of incompetents who make some kind of living by presenting themselves as professionals to unsuspecting proprietors of small firms. Some, for instance, may have worked briefly as paste-up artists for studios or printers and on the strength of this experience offer their services as 'consultants'.

Having avoided a disastrous beginning, and found the best source of design and artwork in your locality, you can now put in hand the layout for your very first press advertisement. Kindly note, however, that from here onwards in this book, for the sake of brevity, the word 'artist' refers to the individual or group you have selected.

Briefing your artist

Inevitably, in the preliminary meetings with your artist you will have described the origins of your firm, your product or service and your plans for the future. During the initial briefing you should repeat the process in greater detail, invite questions and show him the manufacturing process, if there is one. Even if you are selling something highly technical, it is advisable to ensure he has at least an elementary grasp of its use and advantages.

Your ambitions are also of consequence and should be outlined as realistically as possible. The reason is quite simple: if, for example, you intend marketing a new line in a product range, or opening a second shop or introducing an improved version of an established product, the artist can begin to think in terms of a series of advertisements or creating a design that can be adapted easily later on. Such planning in advance will save you money and add continuity to your campaign.

After this general discussion — which will provide a valuable backdrop — you can at last talk about the copy you have written for your press advertisement and explain the reasoning behind it. Illustrations, if wanted, should be described or existing photographs produced for comments.

Although in this chapter we are concerned with a single press advertisement or perhaps a series of them, in practice you would probably also be discussing other components of a complete scheme, including, say, literature, mailing shots and display material. These would almost certainly have a common theme, or at least a number of shared features so that each medium supported the other, but for the sake of simplicity and clarity those considerations will be ignored.

If your artist has been well chosen he may now suggest ideas or offer you sensible guidance based on his experience. Listen carefully to his comments and try to build a partnership from which fresh angles and notions will spring to add excitement and interest to the way in which your advertisements are presented. In some advertising agencies, senior artists and copywriters are encouraged to work as creative teams, from which truly brilliant campaigns sometimes emerge. Although you may be unable to match their special talents, you can still benefit from emulating this co-operative approach.

Costings and fees

During the initial briefing, do remember to give the artist a copy of your press production schedule, and specimen copies of any publications on it with which he is unfamiliar so that he can see the printing standards. This information will help him select an appropriate method of illustration, which in turn may affect his costings, since now is the time to talk about fees.

Armed with all the background knowledge he needs, he can submit a reasonably accurate estimate. However, in order to clarify his thoughts before preparing the quotation, he may wish to produce a rough visual for your comments and his subsequent guidance. To demonstrate your faith in his abilities at this early stage, it might be prudent to offer payment for this exercise whatever the outcome of your negotiations.

Quite apart from the ethics of speculative work, there are sound reasons for advising you to pay. You are trying to establish a relationship with a person who may prove to be an invaluable ally. If, from the very outset, he believes that you are guided by fair principles you will benefit from his immediate trust and enthusiasm.

Naturally, when the estimate is submitted you may need to seek the artist's advice on reducing certain costs to meet your budget. But avoid the error of cutting expenditure so drastically that he is unable to prepare an effective advertisement. In these circumstances it will always be better to cancel or postpone one or two media insertions in order to fund production costs. Note also that at the beginning you may need extra work, such as a logotype design, which will inevitably increase your expenses.

When money matters have been settled you can arrange a timetable with your artist and ask him to prepare a layout. Be sure to discuss copy dates and emphasise that you do not want a last-minute rush.

Checking the layout and artwork

When the layout arrives you should satisfy yourself and your colleagues that this particular approach is appropriate for your firm, your product or service and your market. Ask your artist to confirm that all type matter will be easy to read in the size he has calculated and that the illustrations will be sharp and easily understood, bearing in mind their size and any reproduction problems that may arise. You must be completely convinced that your advertisement is right in every respect. Do not hesitate to ask for a revised layout if you have the slightest doubts.

After approving the layout, every change of mind will be an expensive luxury for which you must be prepared to pay extra. So before returning it, and the copy, to the artist, read every word, check the punctuation and examine every statement to ensure all is exactly as it should appear in the advertisement.

Following approval of the layout you will receive the master artwork. At last your copy is in print, and this is your final chance to check every aspect of the work before material is sent to the publications in which space has been booked. Take your own rough copies on your machine and pass them to colleagues for a final scrutiny, but warn them that, apart from studio errors, every amendment will cost you money. This is no time for a major redraft! Mark errors and essential alterations, if any, on a copy and pass them to the artist who will now prepare suitable material for despatch to the publishers, or supply you with the necessary adaptations for use by your platemakers, depending on the decisions you have reached about how the production will be handled.

Producing your own advertisements

If your artist is fully experienced he may volunteer to handle the production for you, and although you would save about a quarter of the cost by processing the work yourself, it takes a certain amount of time and needs careful attention to detail.

For this reason, delegation might be the wisest course, but since you may have the time to spare, or must save money or your artist cannot help, the following advice will point you in the right direction.

First, you will recall that at the end of Chapter 6 on space buying you were advised to prepare a production schedule showing the copy date of every insertion and the kind of copy required, including exact dimensions. This is now your key document.

As you have learned, advertisement type areas vary in size, and when booking space it is important to appreciate that certain adaptations will cost more than others, depending on whether photographic enlargements or reductions can be used. You should appreciate, then, that when a rectangle is enlarged or reduced by the camera, both dimensions are increased or decreased in the same proportion. Take, for example, a rectangle 6 inches high by 4 inches wide. If you increase the height by 50 per cent it becomes 9 inches, while the width is also increased by 50 per cent to become 6 inches.

It follows, therefore, that if your master artwork is of such proportions that it can be enlarged or reduced photographically to fit the various spaces on your schedule, the adaptation process will cost very little. On the other hand, if you must produce new artwork for every insertion booked the procedure becomes impossibly expensive.

In practice, you must usually compromise between these extremes. The type areas of some publications vary by just a few millimetres, and while the publishers will not accept oversize copy, advertisements can 'float' slightly in one dimension. Thus, if the type area of a quarter-page space is 124mm × 86mm and your master artwork reduces to 124mm × 83mm, this discrepancy will be unnoticed by the reader.

Before producing the master artwork your artist will have considered the dimensions of the various spaces booked as shown in your schedule and will have decided on proportions that give the best compromise. But in some cases the type areas may be such that special adaptations are necessary. This normally involves taking one or more photoprints — sometimes called 'bromides' — from the original and then assembling the components to fit the required dimensions. It may also be necessary to fit special masks to photographs or other illustrations to alter their shapes.

All the additional artwork needed to make your advertisements fit the spaces booked will eventually be supplied by the artist. Now, with the help of a platemaker, you must convert these originals into a form that will be accepted by the publishers.

Working with the platemaker

'Platemaker?', you ask, 'I don't know any platemakers.' But in fact you probably do. Most printers have a platemaking section, and those with reasonably sophisticated equipment can help you. Alternatively they will put you in touch with the nearest independent platemaker or, of course, you can trace him through local directories.

His job will be to supply you with exactly the right material, to the correct size, as described in the publisher's rate card. It will also help if you show him a copy of each publication so that he can judge whether additional work is needed to ensure a high standard of reproduction. He will supply you with either photographic film or photoprints to a particular specification, such as:

(a) Camera-ready artwork (a photoprint from your master)
(b) Negative film, right-reading, emulsion side down
(c) Negatives or screen bromides
(d) Letterpress.

For letterpress you need a metal block which the publishers will make for you from special photoprints or film supplied by your platemaker. There will be a small charge from the publishers for the block, which becomes your property and can be used elsewhere if it is the right size and has the correct half-tone screen.

If your platemaker is efficient you will receive the various pieces of film and photoprints from him, correctly identified and ready for despatch to the publishers. They will probably be supplied individually in transparent bags from which they should not be removed, although you should check the dimensions before sending them to the publications. Address them to the advertisement department and enclose 'copy instructions' which specify the periodical or newspaper, the date of publication, size of space, number of colours and position, your own order number, any special instructions and a copy taken from the master artwork for identification purposes. Always protect film and photoprints for their journey through the post by sandwiching them between sheets of stout card. Never enclose pins or paper clips, which can so easily damage delicate surfaces.

If you have booked space in two or more colours it is essential to send a colour breakdown. Just take a copy from the original, and paint or crayon it very roughly to show how the colours are distributed. Your platemaker will supply separated film, one for each colour, but do remember to specify the actual colour agreed in your space order. For example, on your rough guide you might write very prominently in red ink, '2 colours as booked: black and standard blue, separated as indicated here'.

Full colour insertions need a special procedure. To start with, your platemaker must be able to produce the necessary film and supply proof in colour. The processes and safeguards are so highly technical that you must rely on the guidance of your artist or a printer whose qualifications and expertise are beyond doubt. An 'instant print' shop, supplying simple stationery and literature, would certainly be unsuitable unless the proprietor fully understands the intricacies of full colour work and has long practical experience in the art.

Again, you must refer to the rate card to establish the kind of film required by the publisher and the exact sizes. You will also need colour proof in a specified form. The best advice I can offer is to give your artist or platemaker a copy of the rate card or cards, with instructions to liaise with the publishers.

Whatever the arrangements, you will receive proof in colour from the platemaker and be asked to approve it. Do be reasonable and helpful when making your comments. If exact colour reproduction in parts of the illustration is of little consequence, you will be wise to accept a close match. Look rather for sharpness and the overall effect, although of course where colour values are important you must seek a fair result. Fabrics or special pigments, for example, must obviously be reproduced accurately, but do realise that when your advertisement is printed by the publishers at great speed on mediocre paper and with a deadline to meet, you cannot expect fidelity of a high order.

When you book a full page in black only or in colour, you may be offered 'bleed', which means that the advertisement covers the entire page, and this will affect the size of your type area appreciably. It must be taken into account when preparing the artwork and you should therefore seek advice from your artist. The publisher charges extra for 'bleed' pages, but there are circumstances in which the greater impact they impart to the advertisement fully justifies the additional expense, particularly if facing pages are booked to form a double-page spread or the centre pages are used to give a 'centre spread' in which one unbroken image may occupy two complete pages.

Throughout this chapter I have ignored the restrictions that are often imposed by trade unionists. Most of the national publications and many of the local ones are produced by trade union houses, who sometimes refuse to handle artwork or film from unrecognised sources. The degree of militancy varies and fluctuates. You may therefore deem it wise to consult your suppliers on this matter before giving them work. Because the subject is partly political and thus controversial, I give no firm advice, but you should be aware of the risks to a campaign if your artist or platemaker is 'blacked' at the eleventh hour because they belong to an 'unacceptable' union or to none at all.

Example

Before leaving this cardinal subject of production, let us return to the furniture manufacturers whose advertisement copy we examined in the previous chapter. When briefing the artist they emphasise that every component in the advertisement must suggest the products' outstanding qualities. Headlines, other display type and body matter must be set in faces of roman origin; illustrations must be sharp and well drawn; photographs are unsuitable since they may reproduce badly in local newspapers; discreet and generous disposition of 'white space' in the design will suggest distinction.

The artist shows them specimens of scraper board drawings by one of his colleagues. Although they will be expensive, a high standard of reproduction, even in local newspapers where printing is poor, will be virtually guaranteed and it is agreed that a quotation for the complete campaign shall be submitted. The price is subsequently approved.

Because the artist can supply photoprints with a high order of sharpness from his own darkroom and the local media will accept them as copy, the adaptations are easily processed at low cost, whereas half-tone illustrations would have required more expensive material from the platemaker.

This is a case where attempted economies would almost certainly have resulted in inferior reproduction quite inappropriate to the products advertised and likely, therefore, to damage rather than enhance the advertiser's good name.

Checklist

1. Will an illustration add interest or information to your message?

2. If so, which technique will give the best result in the publications you intend using?
3. Can you afford the cost of colour? If so, what are the benefits?
4. Which type-styles do you favour to support the visual appeal of your message?
5. Before employing your artist, did you investigate every possible candidate, including local studios?
6. Did you consult local printers to investigate your artist's technical knowledge and reliability?
7. Did you give your artist a copy of the press production schedule during the initial briefing?
8. Did you check the copy in great detail before returning it to the artist for artwork?
9. Did you check the master artwork carefully before returning it to the artist for adaptations?
10. Did you discuss the production requirements of each publication with your platemaker?
11. Did you send copy instructions to each journal?

Chapter 10

Testing Copy and Media

When an advertiser initiates a campaign he takes several risks. The publications or other media may be inappropriate. The size of his advertisements or the positions they occupy may be unsuitable. The message, design or concept of the advertisement may be ineffective.

If the advertiser has long experience of using certain publications and can be reasonably sure his choice is correct, it follows that poor results stem either from the size and positions or from the concept and copy. But if he has successfully advertised the same or a very similar product in spaces of equal size and in similar positions, he can be fairly sure that thin response is due entirely to weak copy, unless market conditions have declined.

I say again, every new advertising campaign involves risk. No one, not even the most brilliant advertising agent, can guarantee results. At best an agent may say that previous experience from advertising similar products in parallel circumstances makes him optimistic. Spending a publicity budget therefore requires extreme care, every step being evaluated before proceeding further, and such precautions are especially necessary for small firms with limited funds.

When a press schedule for the year has been compiled, it is advisable to book, say, the first three insertions in each publication and ask advertisement managers to 'pencil in' the remaining spaces as described in Chapter 6. One insertion would be unsafe for test purposes since an allowance must be made for the cumulative effect of a series of advertisements. A national advertiser, depending for results on the sheer weight of a campaign, would regard these limited bookings as derisory. Likewise, if your advertising is addressed to a consumer market you should think in terms of, say, a dozen insertions or more. Obviously such decisions will rest on your common sense and judgement.

If the media on your schedule fall into various categories according, perhaps, to certain markets or groups of prospects, it may be advisable to select just one or two publications from each category and delay booking space in the remainder until the results from these representative newspapers or periodicals are known.

When the main purpose of an advertisement is to pull immediate enquiries, the outcome can be assessed quickly and with some accuracy. Note, however, that the quality of the replies will not be proved until firm orders or new contracts are negotiated. If a heavy response is not converted into profitable business, it would be sensible to check the efficiency of your sales procedures before condemning the copy or media. If, for example, there is a long delay before enquiries are dealt with, or sales staff are unsupervised and have little incentive to follow them up, a poor conversion rate cannot properly be attributed to the advertising.

Clearly, then, publications and advertisements can only be tested if the sales backing is known to be competent.

Monitoring enquiries

Monitoring enquiries is a simple matter when a routine is carefully observed. By inserting a 'key', such as a department or room number, in your address, the journal or periodical from which the enquiry originates can be easily identified. Also, of course, most trade and industrial publications have reader reply services. Every enquiry by telephone should be referred to a designated person who automatically asks the prospect where he or she saw the advertisement. When this information has been logged the business can be dealt with in the normal way.

Although an elementary system such as this is easily arranged, in my experience most firms are much too casual in their attitudes to advertisement replies and one seldom encounters a truly efficient scheme yielding reliable intelligence on which subsequent campaigns can be based. Often, of course, salesmen seek full acclaim for their new business, whereas in fact advertisements may be responsible for many of the introductions.

In contrast, the source of business from mail order advertisements is indisputable. When a reader fills in a coupon which has a key to identify its origin, and encloses a cheque, the value of the publication for this type of selling can be assessed precisely.

Alternatively, again, an advertisement that does not invite an immediate response of some kind is virtually impossible to monitor. Therefore, if copy and media must be tested it will be necessary to invent an offer which will induce either replies or positive action for assessment. A retailer might include a 'money off' coupon in advertisements in a number of different local newspapers and magazines to measure the response from each; a key would identify the source, but even this is not essential since one has only to check the reverse side of a coupon to detect its origin. A manufacturer seeking large, long-term contracts would not expect a quick response and might count himself lucky to receive a few serious enquiries every week. However, to check the pulling power of various publications the sales director could perhaps offer a technical paper or wall charts free of charge.

At the end of a test it will be possible to analyse the value of each insertion by calculating the cost per enquiry and then, if you can trace the history of every transaction, the cost per sale. If the results from just one or two publications are disappointing you can be reasonably sure that the copy is effective, but consistent failure would suggest that the advertisement itself is weak.

Obviously, tests of this nature should be regarded merely as crude indicators of the worth of newspapers or periodicals, and balancing factors should always be taken into account. For example, because in a certain industry the majority of engineers and buyers read journal A you would expect it to yield large numbers of enquiries, whereas journal B might reach a restricted audience of very senior technicians and executives, who might influence the placing of important orders but would not usually respond directly to advertisements.

In another instance, the readers of a newspaper might not respond to an advertisement for, say, very expensive carpets simply because the great majority could not afford them, but clearance and end-of-roll bargains might fall within their average means and attract a great deal of custom.

When a publication has a substantial and verified circulation and regularly carries its full quota of advertisements, you can be sure that the market finds it a worthwhile medium for reaching certain types of people or businesses. If your advertisement fails, there must plainly be a good reason: probably the product does not interest that particular group of readers or your message is unsuitable. To condemn the publication would be unjust, so speak to the advertisement manager who may well offer a solution to your dilemma.

Extending your campaign

As soon as you have confidence in the ability of your campaign to reach and influence the right kinds of prospects and you have established that most of the publications on test are well chosen, you can gradually extend your programme, adjusting the press schedules according to results and experience. Of course, if the advertisement fails to achieve your minimum objectives it must be discarded and an alternative approach found. Take heart from the knowledge that even national advertisers, guided by large agencies, can sometimes produce ineffective campaigns. So ask yourself why your scheme failed, look for obvious reasons and learn from your mistakes. Refer to the rules of advertising explained in Chapter 8. Possibly your sales arguments or their presentation were much too intricate. Try to clarify your thoughts, find a convincing theme and explain it in easy words and sentences. If the product or service is competitive and worth while, and you tell the right people about it in an interesting way that can be quickly grasped, the chances of success are high.

In many cases a press advertisement is merely the first step towards clinching a sale. Sometimes the reader is encouraged to visit a shop or showrooms where he is given a leaflet or booklet; or he may be persuaded to ask a salesman to call and will be offered a brochure during the subsequent meeting; perhaps the reader is asked to write or ring the advertiser direct for sales literature or a data sheet. The role of printed matter in the selling process can be vital, and we shall therefore consider the subject at length in the section that follows.

Checklist

1. For your test have you selected publications that represent the main groups in your press schedule?
2. Have you calculated the cost per enquiry?
3. Have you calculated the cost per sale?
4. Is your monitoring system reliable?
5. If the conversion rate is generally poor, have you checked your follow-up methods?
6. If the results from most of the publications are good, are you arranging to advertise in the remaining ones on your press schedule?
7. If the results are uniformly bad, have you revised the advertisement copy and design?

Part 3

Sales Literature

Chapter 11

Writing Leaflets, Booklets and Catalogues

Writing the copy for press advertisements almost automatically raises the problem of how to convey a full and convincing sales message within a limited space. But when preparing the text for a leaflet or booklet there are usually no such restraints, and a writer is tempted to meander through his subject rather than tell the story briskly.

It is important, then, to appreciate at the outset the need for disciplined composition. In fact, attempting the copy for press advertisements, especially small ones or classifieds, is excellent training. You should also note that the principles of copywriting explained in Chapter 8 apply equally to sales literature production, although, of course, full explanations and complete descriptions can be given.

To produce effective literature the first, essential step is to assemble comprehensive notes on the job, including:

1. A summary of the intended text.
2. A list of benefits to the customer.
3. The photographs or illustrations to be used.
4. A list of photographs, if any, to be taken.
5. A list of drawings or other illustrations, if any, to be prepared.
6. Technical information, such as tables, specifications and performance data.
7. Legal claims or disclaimers.

When preparing a small leaflet for distribution to, say, the public this procedure might be an easy task if there are no technical explanations, whereas the basic work for a catalogue will perhaps take weeks or even months and might require the services of one or more full-time planners. For the sake of clarity, however, I will restrict the advice to copywriting for leaflets and booklets at this stage, with a special section on catalogues later in the chapter.

Preparing the format

From the material you have gathered, the approximate size and number of pages required may become apparent at once, or you should at least gain an inkling of what is needed. A logical arrangement may also suggest itself: for example, in a leaflet announcing a clearance sale of gardening tools and accessories by a hardware store, there might be 10 typical bargains to illustrate and about 50 items to list, giving prices only, with no body copy. These would all fit comfortably on to an A4 sheet (298mm × 210mm), which could be folded once to produce four pages.

For most projects, even at this early stage, it should be possible to arrive at a format of some kind by taking a few sheets of paper and allocating approximate areas for photographs, illustrations, tabulated matter, specifications and other components. The nature and purpose of the job should also suggest where the introduction, descriptive matter and a coupon or order form are to be placed.

You will probably find, as I do, that this early planning is a great help towards finding logical and sensible ideas. If, for example, you decide that a certain dramatic or interesting photograph should appear on the front page, a headline or title may immediately come to mind, and this may even suggest a fundamental theme which can be reflected throughout the copy. But do not worry unduly if notions are elusive at this preparatory stage. From all the facts and material you have collected, it will be possible to start writing a series of sentences and paragraphs which explain the elements of your arguments. Remember to tell the reader what is in it for him or her, and try to think in terms of 'buying reasons' rather than 'selling points'.

It does not matter for the moment if your prose is disjointed and ungrammatical. You are looking for ways of conveying a series of thoughts and ideas so that they are understood even by the dullest prospect. Look for short sentences that create mental pictures. After covering every fact you have listed, including captions to illustrations, put the work to one side and return to it with a fresh mind later on or, better still, the following day.

When you resume you will find that new and better words and phrases come more easily. Now is the time to look for an original approach and adjust your theme and copy accordingly. Seek imaginative headlines that demand attention. Keep paragraphs reasonably short and try to maintain interest by introducing new subjects or angles with brief subheads.

Return to your copy once or twice more to edit, polish and ensure that the sequence of ideas you wish to impart is smooth and easy to follow.

Finally, check your efforts against the rules of advertising in Chapter 8. Even copy testing is advisable before, say, distributing house-to-house circulars on a large scale and, of course, in this case the medium itself should be tested as well.

Using the principles also explained in Chapter 8 you can now count the number of words you have written to calculate the approximate area of type needed to accommodate your copy. The main text is usually set in at least 10 point size, so allow a maximum of 20 words per square inch (say 6 square centimetres). Specifications are sometimes set in a slightly smaller size, and you should count on about 30 words fitting this area. The smallest type you are likely to use is 6 point, which can be read by people with good sight but is often illegible to older readers. It is normally used for disclaimers or unimportant information which the advertiser is obliged to offer. If you must use type in this size, allow 40 words per square inch. I would stress, however, that this method of calculating the type areas required for copy is only a rough guide. Please consult your artist for more accurate reckonings, and remember that typefaces and the space (leading, pronounced ledding) between lines have an important bearing on the cast.

Sales leaflets or folders

The purpose of such literature may be to support the salesman when he calls on prospects at home, in the office or factory, or to augment the efforts of salespeople in the shop or showroom. It may incorporate a coupon, voucher or order form, thus helping the salesman to close a sale, or it may even clinch a sale unaided.

If the product can be seen and closely examined by prospects, the role of a leaflet may be chiefly to add detailed information to the salesman's explanations — perhaps listing and illustrating technical features such as dimensions, materials and components. But when a product cannot be inspected or a service tested, the main function may be to show the reader exactly what he will get, or is likely to get, for his money. For example, although a landscape gardener is obviously unable to produce an accurate picture of a proposed design, he can offer a leaflet, with colour half-tones of previous contracts, to build the householder's confidence in his abilities and service.

Before writing the copy for a leaflet it is important to define its object and try to visualise the role it will perform in the selling process. When pictures play a major part, the captions and text matter should be reduced to a minimum so that the reader's attention is focused on the illustrations. Specifications and supporting data, if needed, should be relegated to the back pages.

If you have only a very brief story to tell on, say, a single sheet of paper, it might be worth using the front for a strong picture with perhaps an attention-seeking headline or statement, and printing detailed text on the reverse. An arrangement such as this, which avoids the trap of spreading a short message evenly over two pages, will add impact and interest to the presentation. Using just one page of a leaflet and leaving the other side blank is inadvisable: not only does it waste a good opportunity for extra publicity at little extra cost, but the white space may be used by recipients for notes or doodles and then discarded.

Leaflets may be folded one or more times in a great variety of ways, and since it is essential to introduce a sales argument in a logical sequence, the several aspects or parts should be allocated to pages and sides in an appropriate order. To arrive at a sensible format you should simply make up a dummy from blank sheets of paper, on which subjects and illustrations can be noted in pencil. The arrangement should then be planned — and amended as often as necessary — by erasing your notes and adjusting the elements until an ideal plan is devised. Do keep the design rational, and above all avoid a format that collapses when the reader picks it up.

Booklets and brochures

When you must impart a considerable volume of information and you want to present it in a way that suggests the subject is of some consequence, a booklet or brochure becomes necessary. It is difficult to differentiate between them: both consist of eight pages or more, stitched together in the centre folds by wire or thread, but whereas the term 'booklet' is widely used to describe printed material of a general nature, 'brochure' is often applied to travel literature or sometimes to suggest a superior kind of booklet.

Many of the principles of writing copy for leaflets and folders apply also to booklets, but because there are more pages the problems associated with holding the reader's interest are greatly increased. When presenting the most important parts of your sales story it is advisable to allow plenty of space and introduce subheads generously to coach the prospect along avenues that might otherwise be rejected. It will help, too, if you support and relieve the text with illustrations and avoid large areas of body copy.

Once again a dummy should be used when debating the distribution of headlines, copy, pictures, charts and drawings. Some elements will claim their natural positions. For example, an exciting title and perhaps an eye-catching picture will be needed for the front cover;

the introduction will appear on an early page, depending on the disposition of illustrations; specifications and tabular matter are normally assigned to the final pages. A centre spread is often used for very large pictures or slabs of colour which can be printed across the centre margin, or 'gutter', as the printer calls it.

Once you have found a fundamental theme for your booklet and established the best positions for various components, the flow of ideas for a title, headlines, subheads and catch-lines will often become almost spontaneous. To this skeleton you can then add the detailed copy, from which an harmonious form will eventually grow. Patience, logic and a determination to find exactly the right words to explain the deal or deals you expound, are probably the most important attributes you will need.

Example

The following example will demonstrate the principles of booklet construction:

An insurance broker decides to produce a small, eight-page booklet which will be offered to the general public in direct mail and press advertising campaigns. The main types of business to be featured in the booklet are:

1. Property and contents insurance.
2. Car insurance.
3. Life assurance contracts, including mortgage protection.
4. Pensions for the self-employed.

A special aspect of the service is that a client decides how much he can afford to pay in equal monthly instalments to cover all these premiums. The broker makes the necessary payments when they become due and consults the client annually to agree how much shall be spent in the year ahead. Variations and adjustments can be made at any time. The purpose of the booklet is to describe the scheme in outline; the reader will be invited to return a reply card on which he or she suggests the date and time for a meeting.

The broker concludes that the ideal page size for his booklet would be 210mm × 148mm, which will fit a standard envelope and is an A4 sheet folded once. From two such sheets he makes up a dummy and numbers the pages one to eight.

Now he can plan the format, and he decides that a line drawing of a house and happy family will be used to suggest the security which comes from the property, contents and car insurances. Likewise, a drawing, in matching style, of mum and dad on a cruise liner will represent some of the benefits to be reaped from the lump sums available when life assurance and pension contracts mature. He then resolves to put these drawings on the front cover — and finds that a title and subtitle spring to mind at once:

SECURITY NOW
The fortunes come later

After some thought and experiment he arrives at the following plan for the remaining pages:

Page 2: A headline only, leading the eye to an introduction on the opposite page (3).
Page 3: Introduction, followed by a brief summary of the proposed deal.
Page 4: A headline, followed by copy about house, contents and car insurances.
Page 5: Copy about life assurance, including mortgage protection, followed by copy on pension contracts.
Page 6: Additional copy about life assurance and pension schemes, including a summary of the advantages and special benefits which can accrue.
Page 7: This is the inside back cover with a corner folded and gummed to form a pocket containing a reply card.
Page 8: Broker's name and address only.

This page-by-page arrangement of a somewhat complex series of propositions allows the broker to present each stage as a simple, self-contained deal which can be understood more easily. If identical contracts were explained in a four-page folder, the layout would inevitably become more cluttered, with various components competing for attention and thus reducing the reader's ability to grasp the scheme as a whole.

Equally, the task of writing the copy is much simplified, and in this particular example the theme suggested by the title on the front cover quickly leads to the following provisional headlines and phrases, which may be revised when the body copy is eventually composed:

Page 1. Pics* (a) House and happy family
(b) Mum and dad on cruise liner

SECURITY NOW
The fortunes come later

Page 2. One monthly sum gives you all this.

*The usual abbreviation for 'picture' or 'illustration'.

Page 3. Introduction
Page 4. SECURITY
At home (copy re property and contents insurance)
and on the move (copy re car insurance)
Sign off: One monthly sum gives you all this
Page 5. SECURITY
Today (copy re life assurance + mortgage protection)
and tomorrow (copy re pension contracts)
Pic: thumb-nail reproduction of house and happy family pic ex front cover.
Page 6. THE FORTUNES COME LATER
When the policy matures (copy re bonuses etc)
and when you retire (copy re lump sum etc ex pension contract)
Sign off: One monthly sum gives you all this
Pic: thumb-nail reproduction of mum and dad pic ex front cover.
Page 7. (inside back cover with pocket)
It's such a sensible scheme we wonder someone didn't think of it sooner!
Front of pocket: Send for details NOW
Front of reply card: Post me today
Page 8. Broker's trading name, address, telephone and telex numbers.

To interpret this format, I suggest you take two A4 sheets of blank paper, fold them into a dummy, number the pages and annotate them as described. See if you can improve on the ideas, but keep everything rudimentary. After this exercise you might perhaps attempt a dummy for an eight-page booklet on a product or service with which you are familiar.

Before leaving this subject, I would mention that if six pages suit you better than eight, the ideal solution may be a sheet which has two parallel folds. If an eight-page arrangement is preferred, the job can be printed on paper or a thin card. The latter is much to be preferred if you need a pocket as described in our example.

Catalogues

Although commercial catalogues usually list all the products available from a company, their purposes vary considerably from attempting to clinch an immediate sale or sales, to providing brief descriptions for professional buyers, who may need very much more information before even contemplating a purchase.

Catalogues addressed to the general public can range from, say, an eight-page list of plants and shrubs available from a local nursery, to the magnificent productions running to many hundreds of pages, all printed in full colour, distributed by large mail order houses. But whatever role a catalogue will play in the marketing process, certain elementary questions must be answered before attempting to plan the format and write the copy:

1. *What, precisely, is the main role of the catalogue?*
   You should be quite clear in your own mind whether you want the reader to call at your premises, order direct from you by post, order from a door-to-door agent or call on a stockist. If the prospect can choose between any two or more of these, you must select the most important alternative and make a clear exhortation to buy in that way. For example, if you sell on a national scale, chiefly through the mail, but customers may also call at your showrooms, the order forms might carry a strong encouragement to 'Post today', which would be repeated elsewhere in the catalogue. The words 'Callers welcome' might be included in an appropriate position but given much less prominence.

2. *How can you convince the prospect?*
   The reader must believe you to be a reputable trader, especially if the terms of business are cash with order. The words you use and the way in which you present and support your arguments will greatly influence his opinion. Extravagant claims, poor design, shoddy illustrations and incompetent printing on cheap paper will suggest products and trading standards to match.

   So regard your catalogue as a shop window from which prospects will judge you, your business methods and, by implication, the merchandise you sell.

   Miss no opportunity to convince and reassure: your money-back guarantee should always be prominently displayed; genuine letters of thanks from happy customers can be reproduced.

3. *How can you persuade the reader to act?*
   Do you want him or her to buy on the strength of illustrations and words in your catalogue alone? In this case your descriptions must be complete and accurate, with powerful reasons and incentives for sending a cheque immediately. Such copy is difficult to write when you are trying to persuade

new customers to buy through the post, although in contrast the loyalties of those who buy this way are unusually strong once they have found a trustworthy supplier.

If the products listed in your catalogue can be bought only from agents or stockists, this vital information must be explained, emphasised and repeated so that the reader fully understands where to buy. A list of suppliers, or at least the name of the local one, must be given.

Special inducements, such as free gifts, may be needed to attract new customers.

4. *Are you seeking regular business?*
If this is your aim, the selling theme and copy style should be adapted accordingly, perhaps emphasising and illustrating the long and favourable relations you have enjoyed with present customers. A friendly, conversational approach will probably be effective, especially if you are selling to enthusiasts.

For example, the retailer who sells a range of fishing tackle and accessories, including items such as special flies that are difficult to find elsewhere, can obviously develop exceptional relationships with his customers. He may send his catalogue to anglers throughout the United Kingdom or even worldwide, perhaps being regarded by many as a good and respected friend.

Building this kind of business by recommendations might take decades, but a good catalogue, suitably written and presented, could achieve the same end within a year or two.

Trade and industrial catalogues

Catalogues produced by those who sell their products to other firms or institutions may have a variety of purposes. A 'short-form' version may be intended mainly as a handy reference for commercial or industrial buyers, who would need detailed information, or possibly tenders running to many pages, on which to base a buying decision. In fact the number of alternative specifications and modifications might be so great that special data sheets and performance illustrations will have to be prepared and typed individually to answer enquiries.

Those, such as office equipment suppliers, who carry a wide range of standard products may expect to sell 'off the page' from time to time, but only then to established customers who know and trust them. The primary function of the catalogue may be to help the salesman when he calls, or to entice customers into the showrooms or give the retailer a ready reference to stocks held by the wholesaler. In the latter instance, a catalogue may be reprinted monthly or quarterly to revise the list of products available and advise retailers of price changes. Alternatively, catalogues may be published less frequently but updated when necessary by printing new price-lists and supplementary literature.

Companies that have produced catalogues for years will usually learn from experience the techniques and systems best suited to their trade or industry and their customers. Sometimes one comes across such a catalogue which can only be described as a relic from our glorious past, apparently having been published annually for decades without changing the format, typefaces or style of illustration. But before decrying this apparent ineptitude you should appreciate that there are many advantages in being a long-established business. Customers are inclined to respect and trust a firm that has survived the recessions and upheavals of our century, and producing publicity material which emphasises a successful history of this kind will therefore exploit a special situation.

Be prepared to adjust the theme, contents and frequency of your catalogues and allied material until you have evolved methods that are exactly right for your market. If you take over a firm which has been trading profitably for many years, be very cautious in your approach to all forms of advertising and particularly the literature. If customers are attracted by the idea of a company's longevity it might be daft and dangerous to wield a new broom.

Data sheets

In addition to sales literature of all kinds, many industrial companies produce data sheets to describe each of their models. Performance details, capacities, construction, materials and compliance with British, European, US or other world standards are explained meticulously, supported where necessary by graphs, charts and illustrations. Specifications are normally very detailed.

Data sheets are compiled by engineers or other specialists to provide technical guidance for prospective users. Quite rightly, there is no attempt to sell. Exaggerated or optimistic claims have no place here and would in any case be quickly detected.

Nevertheless, within these bounds many could be greatly improved to make them easier to read and understand. The need for technical terms and explanations does not excuse verbosity or long, tedious sentences and paragraphs. In fact the opposite will prove more effective: a succinct style leading to a series of brief statements in a logical sequence will remove doubts and so reassure the reader. If bold subheads are used liberally to introduce the various features, a prospect can grasp the total story more easily and yet be able to find and return to specific points immediately.

Good design and typography play an important role in helping the eye unravel the complexities of a data sheet concerned with highly technical products. In all forms of literature the process of informing, convincing and persuading is so much more effective when copy and illustrations are well presented. This topic is discussed in the following chapter.

Checklist

1. Have you defined the purpose of the literature you are about to write?
2. Have you assembled a list of contents, including illustrations?
3. Have you made up a rough dummy and arranged the contents in a logical sequence?
4. Will the cover or front page attract attention?
5. Have you found a basic theme that can be used and repeated in a variety of forms?
6. In your draft copy have you encouraged and maintained interest with good headlines and subheads?
7. Have you checked your copy against the rules of advertising?
8. At this early stage, have you decided on an ideal size? Will it fit a standard envelope?
9. Will your copy fit the approximate areas allocated to text matter?

Chapter 12

Literature Design and Artwork

However brilliant its concept, however clever the choice of shape and dimensions, however ingenious its format, literature design is most certainly a failure if it cannot be printed at a sensible and realistic price. The first, essential rule of literature production is therefore to investigate costs at the earliest possible stage.

Printing costs

If you have followed the advice in my previous chapter, you will have prepared, in addition to your final copy, a dummy showing very roughly the arrangement of various elements such as headlines, pictures, captions, body copy and catch-lines. You will also have some thoughts about the ideal size, remembering that in most cases literature is posted and should therefore fit a standard envelope. You know, too, the approximate number of pages, the kind of illustrations, the number of colours you would prefer and, of course, the quantity needed to fit your immediate and future plans.

From this outline specification your printer will be able to estimate an approximate price. It will be necessary to select a suitable paper or board from samples he will supply, and you may also wish to discuss delivery times if the work is urgent. Listen to his advice about page sizes, folds and any suggestions he may make to reduce your costs. For reasons which will become apparent later in the chapter you should diplomatically refuse his offer of design, artwork or typesetting services, and ask him to quote for supplying paper, for platemaking and for printing only from complete artwork to be supplied by you. If the estimate greatly exceeds your budget you should seek his suggestions on how to cut the figure — perhaps by reducing the quantity or the number of pages, or using a cheaper paper. You may even need to eliminate one or more colours.

At this stage it is important to realise that every piece of literature you distribute acts as your ambassador. There may be cases where a less generous specification is acceptable, but equally your reputation can be positively damaged by printed material that is inferior in design and reproduction. Much depends on your trade or industry and your position in it. Customers are not surprised if a handbill from the local grocer announcing special offers is cheaply produced but, on the other hand, promotion material from a smart hotel or restaurant is expected to reach very high standards indeed.

In extreme circumstances you may be obliged to trim the specification for your work to such a degree that the copy and illustrations must be cut, and after some thought you may find this is feasible.

Layout

Once you are fully satisfied that the printing costs, excluding design and artwork fees, are within your pocket you are in a position to consult your artist about the layout. During the initial briefing he may suggest many ways in which the job can be effectively presented. Almost certainly his imagination and enthusiasm will lead to ideas which are sparkling but expensive to reproduce, and the wisdom of consulting a printer at an early stage then becomes apparent. Otherwise, unaware of the production costs but inspired by the artist's zeal, you might ask for designs based on his expensive ideas. Even worse, you could conceivably be so impressed by the preliminary sketches that you commission artwork, but eventually, on sending it to the printer for a quotation, discover the unacceptable costs. This is the classic recipe for becoming the owner of useless artwork for which you owe a sizeable sum, thus reducing still further the money allocated for printing.

Give the artist as much information about the job as you can. If photographs are required it is advisable to delay the work until a layout has been agreed, since he may suggest special angles or effects. Within the restrictions imposed by your copy and the printing budget, try to give him a free hand. If he makes positive suggestions which will improve the impact of the literature but call for revisions to text or headlines, do encourage this initiative and co-operate if it is within reason. Similarly, if the artist believes he can improve the format without affecting costs appreciably, seek the printer's advice.

Explain to your artist how the literature will be distributed, its purpose and import. If it is just one component of a campaign he must be briefed on the complete scheme so that its effectiveness is increased by repeat copy and design features in the various media.

The value of using just one artist for all your work, including press advertising, now becomes clear. He will be conversant with every aspect of your plans and for this reason can work more intelligently. Moreover, certain features such as drawings, lettering and typesetting will be common to many items in the campaign and, by good organisation at design stage, it will be possible to save considerably on artwork costs, especially if material can be reduced or enlarged photographically to fit the dimensions of other pieces in the scheme.

For example, if the proportions of each are given enough thought during the early drafts, the artwork for a press advertisement might be enlarged to produce a throw-away leaflet. In fact, with modifications the same original could perhaps be used also for printing a window or car sticker or even a small poster. These adaptations might not provide the ideal solution to problems arising during campaign planning, but when a budget is slim and the resulting material is of an acceptable standard, they may provide a realistic compromise.

When you have discussed problems of this kind with your artist and are satisfied he has all the necessary details and background knowledge, including the outline printing specification, you can ask him to supply a rough layout — sometimes called a 'visual' — for your consideration. This will eventually be submitted to you in the form of a dummy, accurate for page size, the positions of folds and the disposition of various elements such as body copy, headlines, illustrations and charts. If more than one colour is specified the artist will indicate where and how it will be employed.

If you are not entirely happy with certain pages or have sound reasons for criticising the complete job, it is very important to ask for revised layouts. There must be absolutely no doubt about every feature of the design, and thus no grounds for later argument or dispute.

Be sure you understand and agree such vital matters as the exact dimensions of the pages, the number of colours and how they will be used, the various illustration techniques involved, stitching, folding, and any unusual requirements which might, for instance, include cut-out shapes, pull-out pages, special mountings or pockets. You should then check that envelopes, if needed, are easily available in the appropriate size. If the literature is to be printed in colour, ask the artist for a sample or an identification number.

Commissioning finished artwork

When you are completely happy with the design and appreciate the artist's intentions in every particular, you should ask him to leave the colour visual with you so that final copy can be checked.

You have now reached a critical time in the production process. First, it is essential to show the design to your printer and ensure it meets very approximately the criteria on which his estimate was based. Any aspects of the job which add significantly to printing costs should be discussed with the artist at once and amended. Now you can seek competitive quotations from three or more printers. This procedure is explained in Chapter 13, but for the sake of simplicity I will assume here that the price submitted by the original printer is acceptable and an order will be placed accordingly.

The second essential step is to ask the printer how the artwork should be prepared. In a general book of this nature a long, highly technical explanation of why this is so important would be of little interest to the reader. Nevertheless, you should know that modern platemaking and printing processes present so many alternatives that only the printer himself will know exactly how the finished artwork should be laid down. The artist will have ideas on the subject, and where elementary jobs are concerned he is unlikely to err. But as the pages increase in number and the arrangement of colour becomes more complex, so the possibility of preparing unsuitable originals increases. In fact, you may conclude that it is safer to ask your artist to liaise directly with the printer and so obviate the chance of your paying extra for subsequent revisions.

The third essential is to supply your artist with final copy which is immaculate in every respect: accurate, complete and well typed so that every word, every figure is readable beyond question. Unbelievably, clients often supply handwritten manuscripts, scraps from other publications or data sheets and even smudged carbon copies on which obscure technical words or tabulated matter are beyond translation. Revisions at proof stage will cost you money which, with care, could be so easily saved.

Having diligently observed these warnings, you are ready to meet the artist once more to put the artwork in hand. If the printer wants it by a specific date in order to meet an urgent deadline, make firm arrangements with the artist at once and offer to help by calling at the studio to approve work in progress or check typesetting before it is pasted in position.

When the artwork is delivered, take copies on your machine and make up one or more dummies to gain some idea of the eventual appearance and impact of the printed work. If overlays on the job make this difficult your artist can overcome the problem quite easily and will supply copies on request.

You have now reached another critical stage. Changing your mind about design or copy will be extremely expensive, and any errors you miss will actually appear on the printed material! So read every word, and check every figure and drawing on the artwork with great care. Then ask a colleague to repeat the process independently. Do not hurry, however great the urgency. Errors or revisions should be marked on the copy taken from the artwork and never on the artwork itself. Do not write on the protective paper overlays if the pen or pencil impressions will be transferred to photographs or other delicate material underneath. Just as important, do not attempt to alter artwork yourself, or ask the printer to do so. In an emergency, ask your artist to call on the printer, where he may be able to carry out minor revisions on the spot if he is told beforehand what is involved.

When the artwork has been corrected or revised it will be ready for the printer, who can now make the plates and run the job in accordance with your instructions. If more than one colour is used he will need either the layout or special instructions on the protective overlays to guide him. Ask your artist to attend to this detail for you and to specify the colours originally agreed.

Until now we have for convenience referred to 'the printer', although, of course, in everyday business one would usually select from three or more, depending on quotations, work standards and reliability. In the chapter that follows we shall examine some of the procedures by which the director or proprietor of a small firm can derive better value from a limited printing budget.

Checklist

1. Have you produced a rough dummy with an approximate specification?
2. Have you consulted your printer about estimated costs?
3. Have you briefed your artist in detail and explained the role of your literature? Is it part of a complete campaign?
4. Did you fully understand every feature of the design before putting artwork in hand?
5. Did you instruct the artist to liaise with the printer before preparing the artwork?
6. Did you supply your artist with immaculate copy correct in every particular?
7. Did you check the finished artwork with great care and ask the artist to supply a colour guide and specification for the printer?

Chapter 13

Print Buying

Large companies and many advertising agencies buy print on such a scale that the employment of specialists is justified. By virtue of their knowledge and experience these buyers save very considerable sums on annual expenditure, amounting to many thousands or millions of pounds.

Although the proprietor of a small business cannot match such expertise or purchasing power, he can still buy wisely if certain fundamental guide-lines are followed. Usually he will know very little about the subject and may not even be familiar with the main processes. Therefore, you may find the following descriptions useful, but I would stress that full technical explanations are far beyond the scope and purpose of this book.

Printing processes

1. *Letterpress*

   Letterpress was once the most widely used process for printing literature, stationery, newspapers and certain kinds of periodicals. Ink is applied to a metallic surface on which there is a raised image. Under suitable pressure, this image is brought into contact with the paper to which the ink is then transferred. The principles of letterpress are demonstrated by a simple rubber stamp, but modern technology has developed the process to a degree of sophistication in which the minute dots of a set of four-colour printing plates can be printed in close register with great accuracy.

   Text and headlines are normally printed from movable type, but illustrations and special lettering require the introduction of metal blocks.

   Enthusiasts claim that letterpress printing still has much to offer for certain kinds of work, but apart from supplying blocks to the few periodicals still printed by the process, you are unlikely to encounter it.

2. *Lithography*

In lithography an image is transferred to the paper from a thin metal plate which has been so treated that ink is accepted by certain areas and rejected by others. In offset lithography a blanket is interposed between plate and paper. Nowadays most jobbing work is printed using this method.

For many years large posters have been printed by lithography, and another variation of the process, web-offset, is widely used for periodical production.

Litho plates are made photographically from complete artwork, with type matter and line drawings mounted in position. The introduction of photo-composition, which is more versatile and has many benefits compared to metal type, has greatly increased the speed and efficiency of artwork assembly.

3. *Thermography*

Die-stamping has long been used to produce embossed lettering and images on paper surfaces. Thermography is a heat process which creates a similar relief effect but usually costs less. Always insist on seeing specimens of the printer's work, to judge the quality before you place an order.

Thermography is conventionally used for stationery, but other applications are possible.

4. *Silk screen printing*

A stencil process widely used for display material of all kinds, especially when short runs are needed or an image must be reproduced on substances unsuited to other printing methods. The process can also be employed on curved surfaces or three-dimensional objects. Silk screen printing is sometimes used for literature production and can be identified by the density and opacity of the image it produces.

Simple stencils are usually cut by hand but intricate artwork must be reproduced from photo-stencils. Body type can be printed by the silk screen process, although the printer's comments should always be sought before briefing your artist and it is important to see work specimens.

The process has been developed in many directions and for many purposes, ranging from overprinting products in the factory to producing large posters. Choose your supplier with care; the small firm round the corner may be ideal for low-cost price tickets or showcards, but quite unsuitable for elaborate displays.

5. *Other processes*
   You may possibly come across other reproduction methods, including photogravure which is sometimes used for printing periodicals when very long runs are needed.

Learn as much as you can about every one of these processes. Your favourite printer will be happy to take you on a tour of his works and answer your questions at any time. Ask about paper, platemaking, colour processes, machining, folding and trimming. Borrow or buy some elementary books on the subject, but do remember that print is a complex topic and you will always do a better deal if you seek your supplier's advice rather than give him rigid instructions.

Seeking quotations

A small firm will probably benefit from limiting the number of printers it uses to three or perhaps four. The little shop in your high street may produce stationery for your internal use very cheaply but is unlikely to be acceptable for promotion material unless the proprietor is a properly trained craftsman. The second supplier might be a firm with modest plant but high work standards; it could probably cope with most of your jobs at reasonable prices. The third company could be somewhat larger and thus able in some instances to quote keenly for the bigger projects. A fourth might be needed for special work such as silk screen printing and producing display material.

Advantages will accrue from building a rapport with these suppliers. Quite apart from making the working relationship more pleasant and enjoyable, it is always reassuring to know that you can count on them for very special service or support if need be. It is wise, therefore, to demonstrate your trust by passing them small jobs without asking for estimates. Naturally they will expect to quote for the larger ones, but once again you can illustrate your understanding by ensuring that tenders are sought on a workmanlike and fair basis.

Once you have agreed the artist's rough layout, take copies from it on your machine and make up one dummy for each printer. With the help of the artist you can mark up these dummies identically to show the following: page sizes when trimmed; folds; perforations; the number of colours and how they are used; headlines; body matter; line drawings; half-tone pictures; bleed and special features such as cut-out shapes.

The dummies should be sent to the printers with an identical letter or memo which specifies quantities required; paper to be used; delivery address and date; how the artwork will be prepared and presented and whether half-tones or other originals must be reduced in different proportions. For comparison purposes, you can also ask about the cost of 'running on' additional quantities. If the job is intricate or you are uncertain about the treatment of certain elements, you should discuss the problems with one of your printers to establish the exact specification beforehand.

When a printer receives scrappy and vague information on which to base a quotation his respect for the client diminishes and the price is increased to allow for contingencies. Furthermore, if he discovers by chance that a competitor has quoted for the same work but on a different footing — and the competitor was awarded the contract — relationships are bound to deteriorate. A reasonable printer will usually be happy to help you draw up a specification if he is given a fair opportunity to estimate for the job.

When the tenders arrive you must balance the prices against other equally important factors. If, for example, the quotations are for a booklet which must reflect the outstanding qualities and reliability of your product, high reproduction standards are essential. Therefore, if the price submitted by one printer exceeds the others by 10 per cent but you believe he will do a better job, you might well be justified in ordering from him. On the other hand, it would be pointless to spend even a pound or two extra on forms or stationery which never leave your factory and so have absolutely no publicity value.

If you receive a quotation that is very much higher or lower than those presented by competing firms for the same work, the discrepancy will be worth investigating. Almost certainly a misunderstanding has arisen, and in fairness the printer should be asked to examine his calculations. You may have misled him in some way.

This system of seeking tenders on an absolutely impartial basis reveals another advantage of commissioning your own, independent artist. Many printers provide a studio service and will often quote very competitively for design work. Superficially, therefore, you would seem to be saving an appreciable sum of money, but in fact, because of copyright restrictions, you are pledging yourself to use that firm for your printing, whatever the cost. Avoid this trap, and avoid too the practice of holding 'auctions' after printers have quoted a price for work based on your specification. It is sometimes tempting to reveal the lowest tender to one of the other suppliers and promise him the contract if he quotes below that figure. But quite apart from matters of dignity and ethics, these tactics eventually become common knowledge among printers in a district, your reputation is damaged and your cries for help in a crisis will be ignored.

Similarly, in the long run it is unwise to ask for designs and ideas on speculative terms. 'Do me a layout and if I like it I'll pay you' is the kind of request that every printer and artist hears from time to time. You should understand, however, that the best people are likely to be much too busy anyway to consider accepting such offers — which they might even judge to be an insult to their abilities and integrity. In consequence only second-class suppliers may agree to the suggestion, and poor design, as we have seen, may ultimately cost you more. In any case, you may believe that arrangements of this kind debase the business standards of both parties.

Print planning

In many, perhaps most, businesses print is bought piecemeal and usually at the very last moment, so that overtime charges are constantly incurred. Often, too, emergency buying means that printers who would supply at lower prices cannot deliver by the specified dates and orders must be passed to their more expensive competitors.

Boasting that you can get a leaflet printed in 24 hours may impress the uninformed, but a truly efficient buyer gives his suppliers plenty of time when he can. In fact, those who are constantly placing business which is desperately urgent have effectively lost control over prices and standards. Of course emergencies do arise occasionally, and if a client normally allows a printer ample time for his work, a genuinely urgent order will be recognised immediately and dealt with sympathetically.

By planning ahead sensibly you can eliminate overtime charges throughout the production chain, from artwork to delivery. When a campaign schedule is prepared well in advance the artist can submit designs for every component, and once the copy and layouts are ready it will save considerable sums if the artwork is put in hand for the complete scheme. Typesetting, photography, copy photography and other elements can be ordered and handled in larger quantities at lower cost. At printing stage, too, multiple machining, as described in the paragraphs that follow, may cut prices.

When layouts are approved, but before artwork is started, you will probably do a better deal if you consult your favourite printer. He may, for instance, be able to suggest a paper which he has bought at a special rate, or in suitable cases you may wish to ask him about machining two or more jobs on the same plate or plates and then trimming them out.

If your designs include two small leaflets and you need the same number of copies of each, to be printed in identical colours on identical paper, your printer could perhaps run them both from a large plate or plates and then trim each to size. But with careful planning it may be possible to extend this principle by arranging several items on one plate. If you want double quantities of one piece, such as an order form, you can simply lay down two identical images. You might even ask your artist to bear these possibilities in mind at design stage and actually plan for them during the initial briefing. I must emphasise very strongly, however, the wisdom of consulting your printer when contemplating these techniques, and of checking the validity of major quotations by seeking competitive estimates.

Another suggestion that may help you to save money on work that is not required at once, is to ask your printers to quote for supplying copies by a certain date, possibly two or three months ahead. They may welcome a contract which allows them to fill gaps in a production programme and so estimate accordingly, but of course to justify such an agreement the job must be of a suitable size.

Before we leave this subject I would submit a plea to you on behalf of legitimate printers everywhere. Good printing demands a mixture of craftsmanship, high technology, art appreciation, an ability to interpret the artist's intentions and an understanding of many allied subjects and materials such as the behaviour of paper and inks. These things cannot be learned in a year or two. Indeed, after a lifetime of study many true printers will say they are still apprentices.

Remember this in your dealings with them. From honesty, respect and loyalty you will gain so very much more than just a lower price or a better job. You will earn the friendship of a very special group of people.

Now, in the following section, we can examine two fields of advertising in which good print buying plays an important part: house-to-house circulars and direct mail advertising.

Checklist

1. Have you ensured that every one of your printers is quoting for work on exactly the same basis?
2. Do you plan your print buying sensibly or are you habitually

paying for overtime work?

3. Can you save money on artwork and printing by planning complete programmes?
4. Will multiple machining save you more?

Part 4

Direct Contact with Prospects

Chapter 14

House-to-House Circulars

Reaching the general public or a specific group of people effectively through press advertisements is not always possible or advisable. You may have a very long story to tell, or it may be important to illustrate a product in full colour; experience may show that people respond better to 'money off' vouchers compared with coupons in advertisements — which prospects must remember to clip; or you may just want to suggest that yours is a person-to-person message.

Making the choice

For these or many other reasons you may decide to investigate using either house-to-house circulars or direct mail advertising. Each has its special merits, to be carefully weighed before reaching a decision on which is best, and in some cases it may be worth testing them both to compare the costs and results. Often, however, common sense will tell us which of the two is likely to be the wisest choice. House-to-house can be used to pin-point certain groups when the territory or type of property is important. If, for example, you want to reach the occupiers of bungalows in particular districts and you can find contractors who will agree to distribute circulars selectively, the problem is easily solved. Likewise, the medium enables you to reach many different categories, such as the owners of pre-war properties who may be interested in home improvements, or people who live in certain areas or roads and are thus likely to belong to a specific social class that you wish to influence, or to receive incomes within defined brackets.

In these and similar ways you can identify and reach special groups of prospects with considerable accuracy or, in contrast, arrange blanket coverage of complete towns, cities or larger areas. The latter technique is frequently used to introduce and create universal interest in new domestic products such as soaps or detergents. Vouchers, and even samples, may be included in the distribution if desired.

House-to-house circulars offer some advantages over postal

advertising: envelopes are not essential, addressing, enclosing and postages are eliminated and the exact date of a 'drop' can be arranged to suit the timing of a publicity programme. Nowadays your circulars can be delivered by the postman.

Circularisation works most effectively when it plays a part in an integrated campaign. As an example, let us consider the director of the glazing company mentioned in Chapter 4. If he decided to limit his publicity to dropping sales leaflets through the letter-boxes of older houses in his district, the response would probably be mediocre. After all, circulars of this kind are commonly received by most families many times during the year. Suppose, however, he took advertisement space in local newspapers to announce that selected households would shortly receive advice on how to increase the value of their properties by more — 'much more' than the 'expected 10 per cent this year'. Such an appeal to the need for greater security felt by most people would attract the eye and interest of many readers. The message on the front of his sales leaflet might say, 'Property values up 10 per cent this year? Yours can increase by more. Much more.' Inside pages might explain this main idea and claim that such benefits as greater comfort, reduced condensation, fuel savings and the other advantages attributed to double glazing therefore come 'free'. The slogan, 'Seeing is believing', and perhaps even such phrases as, 'unbelievably thin', used in previous campaigns, could be retained to ensure continuity.

To its great disadvantage, house-to-house distribution is associated in the minds of many people with the wretched word 'circular', which is so frequently used disparagingly. I have never understood why people describe circulars as a nuisance, and why in recent years a protest movement has been formed in an attempt to ban them. After all, in every home the waste bin is never far away, and I wonder how many of the protestors have in the past used 'money off' vouchers or samples that arrived on their doormats.

Nevertheless, you will be wise to remember these attitudes when writing and producing your house-to-house material. Undoubtedly there are those who view circulars as an intrusion and are likely to react by consigning them immediately to the rubbish tip unless, in a fraction of a second, you can arouse very strong interest.

In future you will, I hope, examine very critically every promotion piece that comes through your door and try to estimate its chances of success. You should first establish what action the originator wants the prospects to take, then assess what hopes there are of the material being read, the degree of conviction that is likely to result and, most important, what incentives there are to respond positively and at once. Of course in some cases the pieces may be preparing the way for a salesman, but this objective apart, you will probably conclude that the majority of 'shots' must fail.

As in other forms of advertising, it is essential therefore to test the effectiveness of your circulars on a modest scale before committing yourself to a massive campaign. Assess as accurately as you can the total cost per enquiry and per sale. Ensure the distribution is supported by activity in at least one other medium and remember you must excite the prospect's interest at the very moment he or she sees the circular.

In contrast with direct mail advertising, follow-up shots are seldom employed in house-to-house programmes. The value of following up is discussed in the next chapter, and there are powerful arguments for planning campaigns in which each household receives two or more circulars. The principles explained apply equally here.

Retailers who are making special offers on a list of products may find house-to-house distribution valuable, especially for sales or during periods when demand is traditionally low. The medium can also be used to deliver 'money off' literature or similar inducements, the redeemed vouchers or coupons being counted to evaluate the impact and effectiveness of your promotion.

The whereabouts of house-to-house distributors can usually be traced from local telephone directories or reference books. Chambers of commerce and other business organisations may also help you find an efficient contractor. It is essential to investigate candidates exhaustively before placing an order and even then you should test the thoroughness of their work by spot checks before entering into further contracts. Most companies are reliable, but much depends on the competence of their supervisors. If you can find someone locally who runs a small firm employing just one or two trustworthy teams, so much the better.

Critics of the medium complain, with justice, that when advertising material is not pushed through letter-boxes completely, criminals may identify households where the occupiers are absent for the day or on holiday. To avoid such criticism, you should insist that distributors deliver your material properly, and this should be a condition of your contract with them.

Checklist

1. Before planning your campaign did you compare the advantages of house-to-house with those of direct mail?

2. Have you defined the distribution area intelligently and accurately?
3. Will your campaign be supported by advertising in other media?
4. Does your circular excite immediate interest?
5. Are you testing your methods on a small scale before proceeding with a mass distribution?
6. Will there be a follow-up distribution?
7. Are you convinced that the distributors will work conscientiously, and how will you check their efficiency?

Chapter 15

Direct Mail Advertising

If the market for your products or services were very limited and consisted of, say, less than 100 prospects, the three most obvious ways of seeking their business would be to call on them, ring them or write. Each of these means of influencing potential customers has advantages and drawbacks. Undoubtedly an interview would be most effective, but what if many of the firms were hundreds of miles away? It could take you months to see them all.

The next best solution might be to phone them, and although a long conversation could perhaps arouse their interest in your proposition, visual evidence of some kind would probably be needed to clinch a deal. Something would therefore be put in the post.

But suppose, before calling or ringing, you sent every prospect a letter and a sales leaflet. In the first place you might arouse enough interest for some of the people to phone you or return a reply card — in which case your status would improve immediately from that of a salesman who seeks the favour of an interview, to a representative with information which a potential client is actually seeking.

Of course the majority of prospects would be unlikely to send for more details, but at least some of them should now be aware of your existence. If the contents of the letter and other material were interesting and well presented, prospects' attitudes towards you should, in fact, be slightly propitious so that your telephone call seeking an interview or perhaps offering to send samples or a catalogue, would be more likely to succeed.

In industrial and commercial markets direct mail advertising is widely enlisted for these purposes: eliciting enquiries, eliminating 'cold' calls by salesmen and introducing services or products direct to buyers. The medium is also extremely accurate and flexible. A few, carefully selected potential customers can be mailed week by week or, in contrast, every prospect in an industry can be reached once, twice of more within just a few days. In an emergency direct mail can be used very quickly to announce, warn or encourage a selected group of people or firms. Additionally, a direct mail message is conveyed in absolute confidence.

Direct mail can also be used for advertising to the general public, if the cost of reaching each prospect is justified by the possibility of high immediate profits per sale, or there is the likelihood of regular profits over an extended period from each customer gained. Home shopping catalogues and book clubs are two obvious examples of the latter.

Because the cost of postage must be added to such other expenses as letter, literature and reply card production, envelopes, addressing, folding and enclosing, it is advisable to test a campaign on a small scale before committing a major part of the budget to an ambitious project. Fortunately, in most instances the cost per reply and of each subsequent sale can be determined with accuracy.

Success in all forms of direct mail advertising depends on three main factors: the suitability of the mailing list, the campaign tactics and the way in which sales arguments are presented. Each must be tested and revised if necessary by means of one or more trial mailings.

Mailing lists

Logically, the first step is to define precisely the people or firms you wish to reach. Even if your market is enormous and difficult to describe in specific terms, you should try to visualise an ideal prospect, around whose circumstances, needs and desires the campaign can be planned and created.

If you are selling, say, electronic instruments which can be used only in oil and petroleum refining, your prospects are easily pinpointed as process control engineers in that industry and directors or engineers in independent companies which advise the industry on processing systems. But how can the insurance broker referred to in Chapter 11 define the people he must influence? Patently, almost every adult requires or might be interested in some form of insurance, family protection or long-term saving. The broker must therefore compose a picture of the kind of prospects most likely to understand the advantages of his scheme and respond to his mailings. He might describe them as husbands or wives between 28 and 45 years old with a total income of £xxx or more, a house valued from £xxx upwards on which a mortgage of at least £xxx is owed, two to four children, and two cars. Husband or wife should also be self-employed or in a job without a pension.

Of course it would be impossible to compile lists of prospects to match this specification, but elementary research should determine the districts and even the roads in which typical families are living. Directories or registers can then be used to build suitable rolls, local authorities and libraries being valuable sources of information.

Lists can also be compiled from trade or industry year-books and the like, but sometimes the names of company directors or specific employees who you wish to reach are not given.

Because, even in business mailings, the great strength of direct mail advertising lies in the appeal of a person-to-person message, it makes sense to address your envelope by name and extend this personal approach to the salutation in your letter. When the number of prospects you must reach is small, the problem of finding names is easily overcome by direct telephoning. Compiling and keeping the list up to date will be an equally simple matter; index cards containing relevant details are usually ideal, or it might be a good idea to keep a dossier on each person or firm. Every mailing, every interview or telephone call, and the results, can then be noted on the card or file to give a complete record of your contacts with each potential customer.

The system can be extended and modified if you are constantly mailing a few, completely different firms or individuals every week or so. Fresh names may perhaps be elicited weekly or monthly by phone, and if these are added to the index you will eventually build a very valuable list which can be mailed several times during the year. When new business results from these mailings, the names of the customers involved should be transferred to the 'active' file and the mailings index revised accordingly.

You can also compile your own lists by arrangement with appropriate sources such as chambers of commerce or trade associations. Sometimes they will offer to include your letter or literature in their own regular mailings to members, in which case you must balance the savings in cost against the merits of sending your own personal message to prospects individually.

Index cards become impractical when thousands of names and addresses are listed, and a simple roll — perhaps with a 'remarks' column — may then become the best solution. If your prime source of information is a directory which lists suitable executives or buyers by name, it will probably pay you to annotate the pages as necessary and work from revised editions when they are published.

Naturally, many of the systems suggested so far can be improved if you own or have access to an appropriate computer or word processor,* when recording and keeping facts up to date become

*Under the Data Protection Act all computerised lists of names and addresses must be registered with the Registrar. If you wish, your Post Office manager will put you in touch with Post Office specialists for authentic advice.

so much easier.

Mailing lists are sometimes available from trade or technical journals. In fact a number of publishing houses produce brochures which catalogue their lists, comprising specialists and managers in many categories in a variety of industries. Usually they can provide a complete mailing service, which includes addressing, folding letters, enclosing and despatching. Lists can also be bought or hired from brokers.

Finally, there are firms which specialise in direct mail advertising. They offer a great many lists — commercial, industrial or general — and they will build special ones to order, as well as advising on every aspect of the medium from campaign planning to the creative approach and despatch. Notes on publishers' mailing services and direct mail companies are given later in the chapter. Meanwhile, it is sufficient to know that, with a little detective work, you can compile your own lists, or, if you can afford them, there are specialists available to do the work for you.

Campaign planning

Direct mail campaigns can be used in so many ways for so many purposes that we can discuss the subject only in the broadest terms. Readers who use the medium extensively will profit from studying other, more specialised works.

When contemplating the ideal mailing list for a specific programme, our first action was to define the people or firms to be reached. Now we must decide precisely what we want them to do: ring to fix an appointment, visit a shop or showroom, place an order or send for literature. We must also consider the kind of material most likely to persuade an average prospect to take the action we require, and how many 'shots' will be needed to achieve this objective. We must then devote some thought to the intervals between those shots.

We have seen that repetition is an essential element of successful advertising; to be fully effective, for instance, press advertisements must be seen and read several times. Equally the power of direct mail depends on prospects receiving more than one approach. A mailing can, of course, play a part in a much larger campaign, providing in some cases the final, most telling encouragement to act — the prospect perhaps being exhorted merely to complete a coupon and return it in the envelope provided.

Direct mail can sometimes be the main or even the only medium in a campaign, although supporting advertisements elsewhere will usually aid recognition and improve results. As a general rule, at least two shots are needed. Indeed, direct mail experts may assert that three is the minimum, but in truth, hard evidence from a test campaign is the only true guide.

One of the strongest reasons for a succession of shots is the opportunity they offer to present a variety of arguments within an overall sales story. If one angle leaves some of the prospects cold, another may work more effectively. Attack from several directions is more likely to succeed, but always within the restrictions imposed by costs, and here we have yet another motive for testing on a modest scale.

If the prospect is to be influenced by a series of different arguments there may be advantages in varying the form that each shot takes. The first might comprise a letter plus a leaflet and reply card, the second a folder printed on board with a tear-off reply card and the third a final reminder on a postcard — with a very strong incentive to act at once. It would be essential to gain immediate recognition by introducing a connecting idea or topic, reinforced perhaps by common colours, design features and slogans or catch-lines.

The principles of campaign planning so far explained are not always followed by companies that advertise nationally. When the name and benefits of a product or service are known in every home and the public are reminded of them regularly, sporadic, single shots may be effective if they are part of a much larger publicity programme. Similarly, although certain publishers and motoring organisations sometimes mail irregularly, they are immediately recognised and can trade on the strength of well-established reputations. A small firm enjoys no such advantages. Its first objective must therefore be to gain the notice and trust of potential customers before even attempting to sell. This is unlikely to be achieved on the evidence presented by just one mailing piece.

Arranging the shots

After devoting some thought to planning the tactics, you should consider the fundamental notion or concept which can reasonably be expected to arouse your prospects' interest and encourage action. The first step, as in every search for ideas, is to list the advantages of your product, but whereas in press advertising or literature production you may legitimately seek an approach that is a self-contained proposition, in direct mail you must try to imagine the effects of a series of related shots arriving unsolicited through the letter-box.

If, for instance, the proprietor of a small garage wished to mail selected householders in his district to improve business generally and sales of second-hand cars in particular, he might conclude that the main theme must emphasise his reliability and high standards. He might therefore decide on the following plan:

Shot 1. To arrive 1 June. Letter explaining trading principles + list of cars for sale + guarantee slip. Slogan 'Drive an honest bargain at Browns' to appear on all three pieces.
Shot 2. To arrive 15 June. Letter describing high standards of guaranteed workmanship on car service and repairs + list of cars for sale. Repeat slogan on both pieces.
Shot 3. To arrive 22 June. Letter outlining generous policy on trade-in deals + list of cars for sale + guarantee slip. Repeat slogan on all three pieces.

Thus the campaign makes four propositions:

1. Buy a second-hand car that is trustworthy.
2. Have your car serviced by trustworthy engineers.
3. Get a fair deal on your trade-in.
4. Get a sound guarantee, with no escape clauses, on both cars and service.

The public are traditionally suspicious of the trading methods and technical abilities of car dealers and their service departments. Logically, therefore, a mailing scheme which underlines a policy of honest and guaranteed trading so deliberately and strongly, but from different angles, would have some chance of success. This plan not only explains the policy but highlights its salient benefits by constant repetition of the slogan, which might be varied in future advertising to 'Drive a better (or fairer or safer) bargain at (or from) Browns'.

Compare this methodical plan of campaign with the haphazard mailing shots which usually emanate from local small firms.

When a mailing programme has a single objective it is still possible — and advisable — to introduce new viewpoints simply because if one inducement fails another may succeed. But it is equally important to weave a common thread, preferably based on the outstanding advantage most likely to attract the prospects' attention and interest. Consider, then, a mailing campaign to directors and office services managers of nearby companies advertising a courier business recently started by three partners. The sole purpose of the campaign is to seek appointments at which their service can be explained. This may include:

1. Regular daily journeys to London. Route can be adjusted to meet clients' individual needs.
2. Items delivered can range from letters to loads up to 50kg.
3. Every driver (ie partner) can be trusted to use his initiative in an emergency, or comply with special instructions (eg 'Give this note to Mr Jones and nobody else').
4. Urgent trips to anywhere in the UK undertaken at short notice by road, rail, sea, air or any combination of these.

The partners believe that the most important aspect of their service from the clients' standpoint is reliability, which springs from an intelligent interpretation of the customer's instructions. These may vary from delivery on a specific day to getting a letter or consignment to a destination by a certain time at all costs. Fundamentally, the partners are selling peace of mind, and this must be the basic theme of their campaign. Within this concept, each mailing piece will be devoted to one or two of the major points they have listed. The following plan is evolved:

1 June. Letter 1. regarding regular London runs.
Briefly mention other services.

8 June. Letter 2. regarding initiative and intelligence.
Briefly mention other services.
Enclose reminder sticker for mounting on or near telephone.

15 June. Letter 3. regarding urgent trips anywhere in the UK.
Briefly mention other services.
Offer London map showing delivery areas.

Now the letters can be written:

Dear Mr Prospect

You probably don't want to be reminded about the worries of sending important documents or parcels to London in a hurry, but how often have yours arrived late?

Undoubtedly the best answer is to employ your own couriers: people with the sense and dedication to ensure they get there safely and on time. Impossible? Expensive? Well, not any more when you share our daily runs.

Occasional or regular deliveries — or collections — of letters, parcels or loads can always be incorporated in our London rounds, which cover a radius of 20 miles from the City. Destinations en route are included.

> You can depend on us, too, for individual journeys anywhere in the UK by road, rail, sea or air: for guaranteed deliveries of collections; for special assignments requiring tact, intelligence and initiative.
>
> Whatever your courier problems, we'll take a load off your mind. So ring xxx now for details.
>
> Yours truly
>
> PS. By arrangement, we can usually carry anything from a letter up to about 50kg.

Follow-up: Letter 2

> Dear Mr Prospect
>
> 'Take this parcel to Mr Jones in Brighton; give it to him personally. He'll inspect the contents. If they are OK ask him to sign this acceptance slip; then take the parcel to this factory address in Crawley. Otherwise bring it back to me immediately.'
>
> Not a job you would entrust to an ordinary delivery firm, but exactly the sort of thing we welcome. It takes a load off your mind, saves you forfeiting an assistant for the day, and you know that if problems arise we have the sense and dedication to ring you.
>
> Of course, we are just as happy with normal deliveries and collections – including our daily London run. Or for special journeys by road, rail, sea or air we are always ready at short notice.
>
> Ring xxx for details now.
>
> Yours truly
>
> PS. The enclosed sticker is for your telephone or near by.

Copy for sticker

> **XYZ COURIERS**
>
> Any time, to anywhere UK
> Letters and parcels up to 50 kg
> Telephone numbers (of partners)
> We take loads off your mind

Follow-up: letter 3

> Dear Mr Prospect
>
> Parcels to Pitlochry
> Documents to Denbigh
> Letters to Lands End
>
> You want them delivered, we'll take them anywhere in the UK. Short notice, weekends, overnight no problems. We can drive there or go by rail, sea or air. Intelligence, tact and dedication come free.
>
> Whatever your courier problem, we lift loads off your mind; in fact even quite large ones, up to 50 kg.
>
> Then, of course, our regular London runs save you lots of money – take a load off your costs.
>
> Ring xxx now for details
>
> Yours truly
>
> PS. We shall be pleased to send you a London map showing our delivery area. Just write or ring for your personal copy.

The letters will be addressed to prospects by name.

These drafts demonstrate several important principles of sales letter composition:

1. The first paragraph must arouse the reader's interest.
2. Letters should be brief and to the point. Four or five short paragraphs are usually ideal.
3. The final paragraph should exhort the reader to act immediately.
4. A postcript gives special emphasis to points you want to underline.
5. A basic theme and careful repetition add impetus to follow-up letters or other material.

Note that the slogan 'We'll take (or lift) a load off your mind' and the words 'dedication', 'sense', 'intelligence' and 'tact' have been deliberately selected to sell the idea of peace of mind. Harassed executives must surely respond if they believe the service will eliminate a source of worry and tension.

I dare say you will now be comparing this advice on writing sales letters with the very long, often complex missives that everyone receives from insurance companies, publishers, motoring organisations and the like. Remember, however, that they are written by specialists with much experience in the art. Often, too, the advertisers depend on huge prizes to hold the reader's attention. You may wonder, as I sometimes do, how many people actually study and absorb the prolific detail contained in these mailings, and whether there might be a case for cutting the copy by a few hundred words.

For a small business, unable to afford such magnificent incentives, the safest path is to keep your letters interesting, easy to grasp and concise. Check your drafts against the rules of advertising explained in Chapter 8 and test your copy on a small scale. In fact, before composing your first letters there may be much to gain from reading the whole of that chapter, since many of the principles apply to letter construction and writing. Your preliminary attempts should contain all the essential components, without being concerned too greatly in these early stages about the order, grammar, style or even the number of paragraphs. Imaginative but sound ideas will eventually spring from a rational assembly of the arguments you have decided to present to the reader.

Never steal a concept from elsewhere or try to adapt one to your own product or service. Crime does not pay, and you will inevitably lose the sparkle, enthusiasm and momentum which come only from your own, original thoughts.

Example

Now we can apply the principles discussed so far in this chapter to the problems facing the supplier of art materials, whose search for fresh ideas and attempts at writing advertisement copy have been described in previous pages.

Direct mail advertising may well prove to be the best medium for reaching and influencing his most important prospects. Press advertisements will be seen by the many business people and amateur artists who buy occasionally in small quantities, and this form of publicity may thus stimulate shop sales appreciably. His mailings, however, must be aimed at the directors and managers of studios, drawing offices and advertising departments of local companies, plus professional artists who practise individually or in groups.

The objective is to persuade them to send for the 'Instantype' book and the XYZ catalogue, thus in many instances breaking the prospects' habit of dealing exclusively with his competitors. If they respond by telephone he will have an immediate opportunity to explain and sell the service he now offers. If they return a reply card he can demonstrate his efficient deliveries by sending the literature at once. He can also ring these prospects later the same day to thank them for their interest and seek an appointment.

This simple plan raises several questions:

1. From which sources can suitable companies and individuals be listed?
2. The mailings will be more effective if they are addressed to prospects by name, but how can they be traced?
3. If many large companies are approached at once, the proprietor may not be able to cope with a heavy response. Should he therefore select a sample of typical prospects for a test mailing? Future activity could then be adjusted to match the time available for developing new business.
4. How many names should there be in this sample?
5. How many follow-ups should there be?
6. How long should the interval be between each?

From these preliminary questions the supplier realises that he has three groups of prospects:

1. Large buyers, such as art studios and bigger drawing offices, who would place, perhaps, two or three orders every week.
2. Regular buyers, typically companies with small drawing offices, who normally need an order of reasonable size every month or so. Some of these prospects will place enough business to justify the cost of occasional deliveries.
3. Infrequent buyers, who do not qualify for the delivery service and must call at the shop for supplies.

Clearly, the first category, comprising about 40 firms, is so important that a special mailing will be needed. The proprietor will also canvass each of these prospects by telephone and persist in his efforts until every one of them has been visited. Direct mail advertising will be employed to support this intensive selling.

In the middle category there are so many companies that the proprietor, a very busy person, will use direct mail to eliminate the time wasted by cold calling.

These decisions lead to two completely different campaigns:

1. DIRECT MAIL ADVERTISING TO LARGE BUYERS

(a) Local directories will be searched thoroughly for suitable firms, each prospect being allocated an index card. If the names of suitable executives cannot be traced, a member of the proprietor's staff will ring for information.

(b) The first shot, a letter, will be timed to arrive on the

Thursday that advertisements first appear in the local press. Purpose: to exhort prospects to ring for the 'Instantype' book.

(c) Second shot, to arrive on the following Tuesday, will comprise a reprint of the press advertisement with additional facts.

(d) The third shot, a letter and a small sample sheet of 'Instantype' for testing, timed to arrive two days later.

The mailing campaign will thus be concentrated into the very short period of eight days. During the following weeks the proprietor will be answering enquiries, fixing appointments and ringing prospects while 'Instantype' is fresh in their minds. Copy for the shots is as follows:

First shot: letter

Dear Mr Prospect

New transfer lettering

Stronger — easier to use — unmatchable value

says studio chief.

With 30 years' experience and a team of 15 artists he ought to know.

You, too, will welcome new 'Instantype', with its range of faces that includes all the popular styles, *plus* 20 exclusive designs unmatchable elsewhere, *plus* ornament sheets, display characters in 10 different colours, and lots more.

See them in the 'Instantype' book. We will gladly send you a copy free of charge and with no obligation.

Just ring me today.

Very truly yours

PS. 'Instantype' sheets and our big range of art and drawing materials, accessories and equipment now reach you faster via our new DAILY delivery service.

Second shot: leaflet

A4 sheet, printed in black and red; folded twice in the conventional fashion to fit a DL envelope.

Front cover: UNMATCHABLE STYLES (red lettering, white ground)

Lift cover to reveal ⅔ A4 portion:

Top panel: UNMATCHABLE VALUE (red lettering, white ground)

Lower panel: UNMATCHABLE SERVICE (red lettering, white ground)

Drop lower panel to reveal ⅔ A4 portion:

Overall printing depicts part of newspaper page with the 'Instantype' advertisement on right. All matter printed in black with bold display lettering overprinted in red on left:

RING XXX TODAY FOR YOUR FREE INSTANTYPE BOOK

Back panel. Notes on the various 'Instantype' display faces used in the leaflet + company name and address + telephone and telex numbers.

Third shot: letter

> Dear Mr Prospect
>
> Without boasting, we'd like to prove a couple of points
>
> Because 'Instantype' costs less that run-of-the-mill lettering systems, you may be doubting its qualities. But after experimenting with the enclosed sample I am sure you will find it stronger, easier to use and almost impossible to crack or damage during transfer.
>
> The value is unmatchable. So are the 20 exclusive designs.
>
> Unmatchable, too, is our new super service: order before 10am from our range of art and drawing materials, accessories and equipment for *guaranteed* delivery same day.
>
> So ring me now for your free 'Instantype' book and the XYZ catalogue. Phone before 10 for delivery today!
>
> Very truly yours
>
> PS. Full 'Instantype' range always available; stocks replenished daily. Note also that for regular customers we will gladly send just one of two sheets without delivery charge.

2. DIRECT MAIL ADVERTISING TO REGULAR BUYERS

The mailing to large buyers must obviously be given priority. Although the number of prospects is small, a great deal of time will be devoted to calling on them, and because these prospective customers are so important to him the proprietor cannot hurry the interviews. Moreover, during the early part of the sales campaign he will be developing new relationships and demonstrating the efficiency of his daily deliveries by supervising every enquiry and order.

He expects a certain amount of new business to result from the press advertising alone, but decides that this mailing to smaller, regular buyers will be timed to start about six weeks after the first insertion. Since the press campaign consists of 13 consecutive weekly spaces, this second mailing will fit neatly into the latter part of the programme.

Much of his time may still be needed to nurse the new, larger accounts, and he therefore decides to compile a comprehensive list of prospects in his area, but mail only 100 names during the first fortnight. After that, he can assess the effectiveness of the shots and adjust the future rate of despatch to fit his diary.

Once again the proprietor searches local directories and realises that he will be unable to trace the firms in his territory with art departments or drawing offices, let alone find the names of managers in charge. However, from their advertisements in these directories, from other publications and with his local knowledge, he can build a list of companies which are likely to employ draughtsmen or artists. For example, in a department store there will surely be a display manager and perhaps also designers and ticket writers; large firms may have artists in their advertising or packaging departments; certain engineering concerns will probably run drawing offices; most printers employ paste-up artists.

Clearly, the proprietor must first build a provisional list using his common sense and special knowledge of the area. A search mailing may then locate prospects.

After further thought he decides on the following procedure:

(a) To every name on the list, send a letter offering a free pack comprising the 'Instantype' book and sample sheets, plus the XYZ catalogue and a voucher for a set of burnishers which will be sent free with the first order. This letter to arrive on a Thursday.
(b) A panel on the top of the letterheading will suggest the letter is circulated to appropriate managers.
(c) Second shot will be the leaflet used in the mailing to large buyers but modified if necessary. This shot to arrive on the following Tuesday.
(d) Brief follow-up letter reminding prospects that the free offer expires when stocks are exhausted. This letter to arrive on the following Thursday.

Note from this plan that a 'search' mailing, used here to find prospects' names, usually works more effectively when there is an incentive to reply. In this case, the main encouragement is the free set of burnishers. Note, too, that the incentive is linked closely to the products since it can only be used to transfer instant lettering. It would be a valuable tool for artists and draughtsmen, but will have no attraction for others.

Copy for the shots is as follows:

First shot: letter

Panel at the top of letterheading (simulated rubber stamp)

Please circulate (tick and pass on)

Studio manager
Display manager
Drawing office manager
Chief buyer

Dear Sirs

New 'Instantype' transfer lettering.
Get to know it; use it; test it.
Completely FREE

Everyone's talking about new 'Instantype', with its full range of popular styles, *plus* 20 exclusive designs unmatchable elsewhere, *plus* ornament sheets, display characters in 10 different colours and lots more. People say it's stronger and easier to use but actually costs less.

But don't take our word for it. Test 'Instantype' for yourself, completely free and with no obligation.

Just ring me on xxx. We will gladly send you a copy of the 'Instantype' book, with sample sheets to test, and the XYZ catalogue of art and drawing materials. You will also receive a voucher entitling you to a FREE set of three 'Instantype' burnishers – for quicker, more accurate transfers – when you place your first order with us for any kind of art supplies we carry.

Very truly yours

PS. Ask about our new delivery service: order before 10am, parcel arrives same day.

Copy for voucher

> **FREE 'INSTANTYPE' BURNISHER SET**
> (Half-tone picture)
>
> Set of three burnishers, scientifically balanced, for easier, quicker, more accurate transfers. One tip specially shaped and coated for large characters; other tips in durable plasticised finish for medium and small lettering or delicate ornaments.
>
> In dust-proof case as illustrated.
>
> Supplied ABSOLUTELY FREE with your first order over £xx for 'Instantype' lettering or any items in the XYZ catalogue.
>
> *Limited offer* only while stocks last.
>
> Company name, address, telephone and telex numbers

Second shot: leaflet

As used for mailing to large buyers, but amend as follows:

(a) Add simulated rubber stamp panel, as letterhead, for circulation to managers.
(b) Revise copy in red on ⅔ A4 'newspaper' panel to read: Ring xxx today for your 'Instantype' book with test samples, XYZ catalogue of art materials and voucher for FREE burnishers.

Third shot: letter

With simulated rubber stamp panel for circulation.

> Dear Sirs
>
> So much easier with 'Instantype'
>
> Everyone says this new lettering system is easier to use, easier on the eye and easier on the pocket. With all the popular faces, plus 20 exclusive designs and lots, lots more, it's unmatchable elsewhere.
>
> So ring today for the 'Instantype' book, with sample sheets for testing, and the XYZ catalogue of art and drawing materials.
>
> Test our new delivery service, too. Phone before 10am, receive your parcel same day.
>
> Very truly yours
>
> PS. *While stocks last* we are still offering the 'Instantype' set of three burnishers FREE with your first order. Ask for details. But please hurry!

Style and timing
You will notice that in these mailings the prospect is exhorted to test the new delivery service by ringing before 10am. As he or she will normally receive and read the message on arrival at the office, the challenge is a strong incentive to act immediately.

Notice also that the proprietor has decided on very rapid timing but in this case the aim is largely to stress the need for quick action to qualify for the free set of burnishers. When a prospect receives the voucher there is a further inducement to respond at once, and it is hoped that the campaign will build and maintain momentum at every stage.

From this plan you will see that timing is of considerable importance in direct mail advertising and can even influence the selling theme. In some campaigns it may be better if the shots arrive on a certain day of the week or month. In others a number of shots in rapid succession can be effective, but conversely, special circumstances may suggest that a more leisurely programme is advisable. There are no rules to follow, but from a hunch, deliberation, inspiration or sheer logic a befitting time schedule will emerge.

The 'Instantype' campaign is an example in which timing encourages immediate response. But if, for instance, the objective of a campaign were to persuade men to visit a local store when they are free on Saturday mornings, a series of shots which always arrived on Friday might be ideal. In contrast, business people are often very busy on Fridays, when they try to clear their desks for the weekend, so that letters which arrive mid-week may in this case prove more effective. If your intention is to persuade prospects to buy on impulse, they may react more favourably at the end of the month when a salary cheque has just been paid into the bank.

Consider such matters at length. Use your imagination and try to place yourself in the shoes of a typical prospect. Consider also the tone of your approach. By all means find words and phrases that build a friendly, informal story. But do create a mental picture of an average customer and write accordingly. In some instances, such as financial advertising, a somewhat punctilious style may be mandatory but, in complete contrast, mail shots to young people might call for expressions and idiom which older folk would not even understand.

Whatever the style, remember to close your letter suitably. 'Yours faithfully' will normally be too formal; 'Yours sincerely' may at times be too friendly. 'Yours truly' is often a sound compromise. In a letter which adopted a mock Victorian manner it might be a good idea to close with the words 'Your obedient servant'.

Before we leave this key subject of sales letter writing, I must emphasise once more the need to seize the prospects' attention with the very first paragraph of your copy and then hold his or her interest until they understand the benefits you are offering. You are most unlikely to succeed if your letter is composed in the dull, uninspired style so widely practised in modern business correspondence. With a little thought and determined experiment, the effectiveness of your mailing shots will be transformed.

Letter presentation and printing

In common with every form of advertising, the layout of your letters is of enormous consequence. First, they must look easy to read, with good margins of white space and short paragraphs, so that the eye is encouraged to scan the first few words and then read on. Second, a letter's position on the page will enhance its appearance and appeal; the message must be carefully framed, rather like a picture, with roughly equal borders on each side and a margin at the bottom which is generous but not so deep that the balance is ruined. Avoid an arrangement which spreads the type matter over a wide measure and in consequence produces a ridiculously deep margin at the foot. On an A4 sheet the width of a type area should be about 5½ inches (14cm) at the most.

Careless or haphazard layouts are poor advertisements.

So work at the presentation. Ask your typist to produce a first draft complete with a fictitious address, to give a better impression of the letter's final appearance. Examine it with her and adjust the line width if necessary. Then, if the letterheading allows, ensure the left-hand edge of the typematter is aligned with a prominent feature such as the left-hand side of your company name or logotype. Now retype the letter and examine the right-hand edge of the typing. Will the letter's design be enhanced by taking a word over here or a word back there? Eliminate every 'widow' — the typographer's term for a single word, or two short words, running over at the end of a paragraph to form a very short line. Sometimes the problem is solved by just taking a series of single words back to the previous lines. But failing this, you may be able to edit the copy so that a word of two is added or lost. Be very fussy and critical.

Of course there is much to be gained from applying these principles of good layout to your everyday letters. The standards of presentation, particularly by small firms, are often appalling and inexcusable when a trained typist is employed.

Having found the perfect layout for your sales letters you must now devote some thought to their production in bulk. If the mailing list is short, comprising say 50 names, the best solution will probably be to type them individually and instruct the typist to make every one perfect, without obvious erasures. They can then be signed individually before despatch.

Overcome the temptation to print the letters on your copying machine, however well it may reproduce. No one will be fooled, especially when you match in addresses and salutations with your typewriter.

The alternative to typing the letters is to use a word processor which will, of course, ensure excellent reproduction with the prospect's name and address included. If direct mail advertising plays a major part in the development of your business, you may perhaps decide to buy or hire your own processor. Otherwise, you can find a local contractor, but do check the quality of his work and insist that you see proofs for checking and amending copy and layout, before he proceeds with the run. Even then, it might be wise to examine work in progress to make sure that standards are being maintained.

If your mailing list is so long that using a word processor becomes too expensive, the best solution may be to consult a local company that specialises in direct mail advertising. Listen well to their advice, which will be based on expertise and long experience.

Never attempt a mass mailing of letters which have been reproduced in their thousands by a printer, unless a test campaign has proved the shots to be effective. Never attempt to 'match in' the addresses and salutations on printed letters, since the result is bound to be poor.

Addressing and despatch

Envelopes, of course, will be addressed by the person, processor or firm that types your letters.

Newcomers to direct mail advertising seldom realise that the envelopes used for a campaign are extremely important. In most cases, except where a secretary opens the mail, an envelope is the first component that is likely to influence the prospect's opinion of you and your message. If the address is neatly typed and the envelope itself suggests that the contents are of some consequence, a favourable attitude is created even before the letter is seen. Contrast this with the reception awarded to the majority of circulars, which arrive in the cheapest manila envelopes on which labels are mounted askew.

Surely you would never allow your representative to visit customers untidily dressed in clothes of the lowest quality. Likewise, your letters to prospective customers must never be clad so thoughtlessly. Quite apart from the unfavourable reactions that may result, the shot will be recognised as an advertisement and perhaps dropped into the 'out' tray for an assistant to read.

So, however convenient they may be, avoid labels and manila stationery. Use the best quality envelopes you can afford and be sure they match your letterheadings. If you employ a mailing house, always insist that these rules are observed. Your advertising is more effective when it differs from the rest. Always aim for higher standards.

This maxim applies equally to preparation and despatch. When small numbers of letters are folded by hand, make sure the job is done neatly, that envelope flaps are properly sealed and postage stamps, if used, are mounted squarely. Casual attention to detail may suggest to prospects that your attitudes in general are careless.

If you have large quantities to fold, your printer will probably do the job for you at low cost, to generate goodwill. He may offer, too, to enclose the material in your envelopes, and despatch them if you pay for the postage in advance.

Envelopes overprinted with your business name and address will usually be returned by the Post Office if prospects have moved or 'gone away', although for second class mail they have no obligation to do so. Such returns will help you keep your mailing lists accurate, but do ensure that the overprinting is well designed and produced in order to create favourable first impressions.

Direct mail specialists

A large-scale campaign will need the services of a company that specialises in the medium. Such firms vary from small teams — perhaps man and wife — to large concerns with the staff and very latest equipment for handling mammoth direct mail programmes. The bigger ones are unlikely to be interested in mailing to a list of modest length, and indeed might find that kind of job unprofitable. Circumstances can vary, however, and if you investigate direct mail houses in your area you should certainly speak to them all.

During these researches you may encounter brokers from whom you can rent or buy suitable lists. Before entering a contract with them, do question the authenticity of lists on offer and particularly their age, since they can quickly become inaccurate. Some are compiled from directories and similar sources; others comprise the names of people who have responded to advertisements or special promotions. Accredited brokers will usually give a refund for returned letters and you can, of course, test the validity of a list by mailing a random sample.

Direct mail companies will probably give you a booklet which outlines their services and describes their standard lists. Most will also plan your campaign, build new lists if necessary, prepare creative proposals, attend to the production — including print — and despatch on the agreed dates. They will submit estimates and adjust the scheme to fit your budget. You are always required to pay the postage in advance.

Undoubtedly most of these companies will give sound advice which comes from long practice in using the medium. If direct mail is important to you, and your finances permit, there is an excellent argument for using their services. But when an appropriation is low you must obviously make every pound count by organising your own projects until expansion allows you to delegate the work.

Remember also that the manager of your local post office will be pleased to help and advise you, and can put you in touch with the direct mail specialists in London. They usually give financial incentives to those who are using the medium for the first time, and can in turn put you in touch with such organisations as the Direct Mail Producers' Association, the Direct Mail Sales Bureau, the British Direct Marketing Association and the British List Brokers' Association. Every one of these associations will be pleased to help you.

Publishers' mailing services

Publishers' mailing lists, mentioned earlier in the chapter, can be a convenient means of reaching prospects who are employed in a variety of jobs in many different trades and industries. Some of the larger publishers produce very detailed booklets which itemise their lists and describe the services they offer. If you sell to the markets they cover, it would be sensible to investigate the advantages and approximate cost of using their resources. You should, however, establish whether the mechanics involved can be adapted to meet your special needs. Will they address envelopes supplied by you? Will they guarantee to mail the shots on the day you specify? If your campaign involves distributing just one printed piece, such as a leaflet or folder, will it be cheaper and equally effective to enclose it as a loose insert in the appropriate journal?

The great advantage of employing a publisher's list is the opportunity it presents to support your press campaign in specific journals with accuracy and very little waste. Your letters will reach virtually every reader — a benefit that might outweigh the drawbacks.

When a publisher's representative calls to discuss space bookings, ask whether a mailing list service is available and how it might be a means of increasing the impact of your advertising to selected groups.

Assessing the value of a mailing campaign

In many instances a mailing campaign encourages prospects to take a course of action which the advertiser will monitor automatically. He will know exactly how many people returned vouchers, or sent for details. He may also know the volume of business generated by a mailing scheme, and from this intelligence it is a simple matter to calculate the cost per sale and decide whether the investment in time and money was justified.

But there will be certain circumstances in which an accurate assessment is impossible. A retailer, for example, may merely be able to say that sales of the lines advertised accelerated appreciably; or a manufacturer might find that salesmen were receiving many more enquiries than usual about the products featured in a mailing programme. Typically, too, a substantial number of customers might not admit that their orders resulted directly from an advertisement. Also, of course, the purpose of a mailing might be to influence future decisions if a specific need arises, such as in the case of a car windscreen replacement service or emergency plumbing.

There are hundreds of similar possibilities. The retailer can calculate the sales of advertised goods, but how does he assess the additional turnover which results from impulse buying once prospects are enticed to his premises? In any business, how do you estimate the future value of every new customer gained?

Therefore, if you wish to appraise the effectiveness of a direct mail programme it will be necessary to seek replies in a form that can be counted. Vouchers, coupons, special deals or similar incentives are the conventional answers, but there are many alternatives depending on your trade, industry or sphere of business. Thus, although profitable trading may not result at once from the inducements on offer, the daily and final scores will give at least some measure of the operation's success. For instance, an electrical contractor might judge his mailing campaign to builders a good investment if 20 per cent phoned for copies of his booklet on the latest, low-cost ring main systems approved by the CEGB, although orders might not be placed by new clients for months ahead.

The inexperienced sometimes look for magic numbers with which to gauge the results of a mailing project. 'Surely,' they will say, 'enquiries from 10 per cent of the list must be good.' Or they may complain that 1 per cent is far too low. On most occasions such comments are justified, but what if none of the 10 per cent places any business, and the one in a hundred eventually signs very lucrative, long-term contracts?

Only you, the proprietor or director, can assess the true worth of a campaign, and that assessment must be based on the net gain. A heavy response, massive turnover or a flood of activity are of no avail until they yield commensurate profits.

Likewise, beginners are sometimes dismayed by the number of returned letters they receive from their mailings and may complain forcibly if a mailing house or broker has supplied the list. But again, numbers can deceive. When the only source of information is a directory published infrequently by a professional body which refuses to co-operate with advertisers, the list will certainly be inaccurate after a year or more: people die, move, resign or are sacked. In these circumstances 5 per cent might be a surprisingly low figure. On the other hand, a list which has recently been checked and revised by a trade association might prove almost entirely correct.

Deriving the greatest benefits from direct mail

I would emphasise once more the importance of exploiting direct mail's unique person-to-person appeal. Of course there are occasions on which a campaign comprising just a single leaflet, without even a supporting letter, may be proved by tests to be justified. But speaking generally, the medium works more effectively when the prospect receives a message which has a personal salutation, is written in suitably cordial terms and signed by the advertiser.

Used skilfully and with thought, direct mail has a great deal to offer the small business. With a well-designed letterhead printed on good paper, matching envelopes, a typewriter and a sheet of postage stamps, anyone can become an advertiser. For a few pounds those who run humble, unknown firms can reach and influence executives in international companies. No other medium provides so many opportunities at such low cost. No other medium is so accurate. No other medium can place your name and message on the desks of important potential customers overnight with so little waste circulation.

Its value as a medium with very special, personal appeal is exceeded only by the one which actually encourages prospects to visit you and your colleagues, to view the latest developments, examine and discuss your product or service in the finest detail and perhaps place an immediate order. I refer, of course, to exhibitions and shows, which for many small firms are the highlights of their marketing year, and are the subject of my next chapter.

Checklist

1. How many direct sales or conversions will you need to justify the cost of stationery, printing, postage and despatch?
2. Have you accurately defined the people or firms you wish to reach?
3. Have you investigated the best source or sources for your list? Will a 'search' mailing help?
4. How many shots will you need? Have you considered the timing?
5. Have you assembled a list of the various benefits that prospects will gain from your product or service?
6. If you are using other media, can you introduce a common theme?
7. Can you find a different angle for each shot within an overall concept?
8. Have you checked your copy against the rules of advertising?
9. Have you offered prospects strong reasons for acting immediately?
10. How will you close your letters? Would a postscript emphasise an important benefit?
11. Is the layout of your letter sensible and attractive? Does the letter look easy to read?
12. What steps are you taking to ensure that your letters are typed to a high standard?
13. Are your envelopes well selected to match your letterhead or create favourable first impressions?
14. If you intend employing direct mail specialists or a publisher's services, have you investigated every available source?
15. What steps are you taking to monitor the success of your campaign?

Chapter 16

Exhibitions

Every trade, every industry, enjoys the opportunities to learn, appraise and sell which arise several times a year in international, national and local shows and exhibitions. To everyone these present much more than just a forum or market-place. Within the space of a few days, long-standing friendships are nourished, new ones made, additional sources of supply and information are discovered, the latest trends, ideas or products discussed, trade attitudes defined, innovations unveiled and fresh markets revealed.

For enquiring, progressive business people an exhibition's value cannot be paralleled. For small firms they are a means of gaining general publicity and of meeting buyers or specifiers who will actually be seeking information, looking for new products or services and perhaps placing orders on the spot. Exhibitors can speak to senior executives who might otherwise be very difficult to meet, or spend 30 minutes with them instead of 10. Discussions are pursued in a relaxed, informal mood, without interruption from staff or telephones. Displays, video equipment and supporting material are also on hand when needed for explanations or descriptions.

If exhibitions are attended by the general public, a manufacturer has a unique chance to speak direct to large numbers of ultimate buyers to test their attitudes and seek opinions.

Exhibitions bring companies into intimate contact with their markets. Often they are used to launch new products or enterprises. Exhibition previews and features are commonly published in relevant journals or magazines, and the really big national shows organised for the car, boat and similar industries are widely reported in the press and on television and radio.

Remember, therefore, when planning to launch something new, the special advantages which may accrue from introducing it at an important exhibition. If interest is aroused by mailings, or by press advertisements in exhibition numbers just prior to the show, prospects can actually examine and discuss the innovation with you and your colleagues on your stand while it still has news value. Arranging and keeping an equal number of appointments at other times might take you months.

From these observations you will begin to appreciate the arguments in favour of using press advertising, direct mail and other forms of publicity to back your appearance at the main exhibitions of the year. But whether or not you should take space in the exhibition catalogue is a matter for debate. Your company name and stand number will be listed and almost certainly the publishers will allow you a specified number of words in the editorial columns to describe your exhibits. It is unlikely that visitors will have time during their tours to study the catalogue in detail, and the benefits of an advertisement will probably not be gained until after the show, when the literature acquired is examined during the evening at an hotel or on the return journey. Exhibition catalogues are often kept as a source of reference for the ensuing year, and may thus also offer some reminder value.

Exhibitions provide excellent reasons for writing to customers and prospects both before and after the event. A letter describing your exhibits, or a note that thanks them for their interest and reminds them about salient advantages or features, will certainly build goodwill and may produce more tangible results.

Your display area

If you are considering the possibility of taking a stand at a show for the first time, the initial step must obviously be to ring or write to the organisers for details. If you cannot trace them, the editor of a periodical closely associated with the trade or industry concerned will be pleased to advise you. Some exhibitions are actually run by publishing houses.

Eventually you will receive the information you need including, perhaps, projected attendance figures and relevant statistics, a site layout, notes showing which stands are already booked and the rents of those still available. If you decide to take the matter further, the first, vital task is to select the most suitable position by trying to imagine how an average visitor will circulate, taking into account the location of the entrance, refreshment areas, lavatories and central features, if any. Remember, too, it is very likely that a major stand will be occupied by an important and powerful advertiser who will attract large numbers of people. A small stand near by may win much more attention than others of the same size elsewhere and can thus more than justify a higher rent.

Use your common sense to select the site that best suits your purpose and pocket, but do understand that in general you get what you pay for. You may gain appreciably from spending a little extra, although in a small exhibition position is unimportant since visitors may circulate several times during their stay.

Before deciding to participate, however, you should investigate the approximate cost of building and furnishing your stand. Nowadays, many organisers provide a complete 'shell' constructed to a standard design. You, the exhibitor, are responsible merely for the contents of the shell, including displays, furniture and lighting. Even your company name on the facia may be signwritten for you — perhaps in a mandatory colour and style.

In most exhibitions the fabrication and erection of stands, electrical wiring and the like must be carried out by trade unionists in specific categories, and failure to employ suitable people might easily result in stoppages. So refer to the organisers' literature for guidance on this sensitive topic and be sure of your ground before planning money-saving DIY measures. Almost certainly they will be banned!

Before booking a stand it is also important to investigate everything that is likely to affect your intentions. For example, certain exhibits might require additional electricity, you could perhaps need water or gas, or your equipment might be so heavy that the floor would need additional support. Most of your questions will be answered by the organisers' literature, but failing this be sure to make enquiries before signing a contract.

If the organisers are not providing a shell scheme, or if you must furnish a large area within a shell, you will require the services of an exhibition contractor. First, however, you should list everything you will need on the stand, from actual exhibits to such mundane items as a waste bin or a cupboard for your personal effects and papers. A very small stand will usually restrict the design opportunities to such a degree that a purely functional arrangement is the only sensible solution. Competitive quotations from, say, three contractors could therefore be sought without reference to an artist since there will be little scope for design ideas. Most contractors have their own studios and will happily submit rough drawings with their estimates.

On the other hand, if the site and your exhibits will allow an imaginative presentation, or you are furnishing a large shell, it will probably pay you to enlist a stand designer, or you may find that your artist or one of his colleagues has experience in the subject. If your budget is modest, be sure to warn him that you are seeking only a design service, otherwise he may assume that the construction is to be supervised, for which a substantial fee would be charged. From his sketches and specification you can seek competitive quotations from contractors, but before placing an order with the successful bidder it is important to examine his terms of business. You will normally find that structure and contents are on hire only, so that if you think a certain display piece will be useful for a second show later in the year, or it would fit your showroom perfectly, make suitable arrangements before signing the agreement.

Most small firms, however, will book stands of moderate size in shell schemes and must therefore solve the problem of how to furnish a restricted area attractively at reasonable cost. The best answer is often to buy your own portable display units which are available in many different forms from a number of suppliers.

Modern portable displays are easily adapted to meet special needs; they can be extended if necessary in the future and include a great variety of pieces. In most cases they are easily collapsed for transport by van or even in the boot of a car. When not being used at exhibitions they can be stored in a small space or erected in a reception area or showroom.

Add brilliance to your displays by fixing spotlights and other lighting accessories, but do enquire about the position of power points well before an exhibition so that suitable extension leads can be fitted and concealed.

A great advantage of using portable display units is the ease with which they can be prepared by your own artist long before the show begins; photographs and exhibits can be mounted, captions typeset and headlines lettered. They can be assembled, checked and revised whenever convenient, without incurring costly overtime charges if your artist is briefed well in advance.

If you expect to engage visitors in long conversations, and space permits, try to provide a small office or at least a partially screened area formed, perhaps, by one or two tall units. Note, too, that chairs and a small table are extremely useful, and are especially welcomed by visitors who may have been walking or standing for an hour or more. Finally, keep your displays clean and tidy at all times; use your duster regularly and ensure there is always someone on the stand to welcome established customers and new prospects alike.

If needed, a telephone can usually be installed on your stand in a larger show but do investigate costs beforehand and ensure the dial can be locked when the site is unattended. A visitors' book, too, will be useful for recording the names of important guests, especially if you intend mailing them afterwards.

Come prepared for many hours on duty. If you have sufficient staff, a roster would be the obvious solution to manning problems.

Plan such matters carefully in advance, and check your stocks of literature and samples well before the exhibition so that fresh supplies can be ordered if necessary.

Between shows it may be feasible to put your portable displays to good use by organising a series of miniature exhibitions in hotels or small halls. If your trade or industry is suitable, the possibilities can be boundless. It might even be practicable to work closely with other, non-competing firms and arrange, with shared costs, a tour of towns or cities; or you might go it alone locally. If the business potential warrants such an outlay, prospects can be greeted with refreshments or drinks; you can also offer live demonstrations, video presentations or even entertainment.

From my own experience I can confirm the success achieved by a small team which sold X-ray equipment to dentists, a home improvements company that regularly promoted its products in local halls, and a musician who sold home organs by putting on his own show free of charge in a variety of venues.

With a little thought, a pinch of initiative and pounds of energy, exhibitions can be exploited in many ways to entice visitors to come and see your wares. You may believe that people who make a special journey to meet you must be very valuable prospects indeed.

Checklist

1. Have you listed the main exhibitions that are likely to be of value to you during the coming year?
2. How many of these exhibitions will be shell schemes?
3. Should the launch of your new product or service tie in with an exhibition date?
4. Should your direct mail or press advertising be timed to support your participation in certain shows?
5. Have you selected the position of your stand carefully, bearing in mind the busiest areas?
6. Are you seeking quotations from contractors for this and future exhibitions in good time, so that overtime charges are avoided?
7. Would a portable display serve you better? If so, have you arranged for suitable lighting?
8. Before ordering a portable display, did you consider its other possible uses: in your reception area, showrooms or your own miniature exhibitions?

Part 5

Other Media

Chapter 17

Display Material

Retail displays

The purpose of such material may simply be to remind the public about a product or service as they pass shop windows, gaze into them, or when they are in the shop or store itself. In each case the message must be brief, easy to understand and echo the theme of advertisements in other media so that the prospect recalls or recognises your name or brand. The material may include tickets, small posters, showcards, shelf strips, three-dimensional pieces — which are sometimes illuminated — or displays that have a merchandising value, such as dispensers or stands, and are usually supplied as part of a deal to encourage retailers to buy large quantities.

If you sell to retailers and believe that display material in some form will either encourage them to stock your products or increase sales, you should certainly investigate the idea, but proceed cautiously before committing yourself to high expenditure. First, you must remember that most shops have very little room to spare for these items, and that normally the manager or proprietor will find space for you only if there is a business advantage to be gained. The national companies frequently offer incentives, such as discounts or free merchandise, to retailers who put special displays in their windows or on their shelves or counters.

It follows, therefore, that you must either give the shopkeeper something that is useful or find a deal of some kind that will encourage him to co-operate. The partners referred to in Chapter 8 who manufacture chairs, settees and stools, would have little difficulty in persuading their stockists to set up impressive window and interior displays because the furniture itself will enhance the retailer's reputation, and in any case he will be anxious to derive benefits from a direct link with the local press advertising.

In contrast, consider the problems encountered by a small company that sells meat pies and similar products to delicatessens, grocers and pubs. The windows, shelves, walls or counters of these outlets overflow with goods and displays. Salesmen and merchandisers from the national concerns compete with each other for space. Such circumstances call for more than just the conventional window stickers or showcards. Almost certainly, however, a display with a small built-in battery clock would be accepted by retailers or publicans, and might be offered to those with a monthly turnover exceeding a specified sum. Obviously it is better to spend the budget on fewer outlets and ensure premier long-term positions than produce material in large quantities that will never be placed. But suppose the pie manufacturer wants some extra, supporting units, or is unable to afford the clock displays despite the low price of modern battery movements. He might then consider producing plates in pottery, or perhaps in a suitable card or board, with a slogan or catch-line on a specially designed, abnormally wide brim. The plate could be used to display the large pies that are cut and sold in portions, and again this is just the kind of useful accessory which retailers will welcome and put into service immediately.

Even in massive companies with national distribution of many different products and the marketing expertise to match, indifferent display material is sometimes produced. But small firms cannot afford such errors, so think long and hard before reaching a decision; then discuss it with retailers and test the idea on a restricted scale before spending extravagantly.

Although the medium in its retail applications is essentially a means of reminding the public and therefore works most efficiently when the copy is limited to a few words, there are circumstances in which a longer message can be justified. For example, an unusual tool may require a showcard that explains how it works; a promise or guarantee might be displayed on a ticket or poster, or quotes from press reviews might be printed on an imitation scroll for display next to a book.

Mark also that where customers are obliged to wait or stand for a while, as for example in an order office or reception room, a long message may be studied more than once by captive readers.

Producing display material in quantities large or small will usually call for the services of your artist and printers unless complex assemblies are envisaged, when you may need the help of specialists. So, having decided on the purpose of your project, noted the various comments on copywriting contained in this chapter and written the words to be employed, you should try to visualise the ideal structure of your display. For example, in the case of a showcard, will you need a platform for the product? Should there be a collapsible rudder strut with hanging cord so that the display can be either free-standing or hung? Should you run some extra copies on paper for use as posters? What shape and size should the display be: flat or three-dimensional? Where will it be used? What will the retailers' reaction be? Should it be printed on paper, card, board, rigid plastic, flexible plastic? How many colours will there be? Retailers are rarely happy with displays that are mounted by means of an adhesive on to windows, walls or tills because they can be difficult to remove. What alternative methods of fixing are there?

When these and similar questions have been answered you will be able to scribble something on paper to discuss with your printer. If only a few copies are involved, or you propose using materials other than paper, board or card, the silk screen process will be the obvious choice. Large quantities or full colour reproduction will probably call for lithography.

After this initial meeting with your printer, and having confirmed that the job is roughly within your budget, you can safely talk about it with your artist and ask him to prepare a dummy for further discussion. If, when it arrives, you have the slightest doubt about retailers accepting the display, seek comments and guidance from selected shop proprietors and managers. Display the dummy in one or more typical sites to judge whether it is prominent enough and easily understood. Ask yourself whether, in competition with other pieces, it demands attention and creates interest. If satisfied, you can order the artwork and printing in the usual way, but unless you are completely confident of the project's success, do order a minimum quantity for testing.

Trade and industrial displays

Unlike retail display material, displays for trade or industrial promotions are often produced in very limited numbers but are usually more intricate. Typically, a small business which sells its products to other firms or establishments in the UK might need one large, free-standing permanent display for its own reception room and, say, four duplicates for its main agents in the provinces.

Assuming that each display consists of a standard, portable unit with photographs, captions, one major headline, 50 words of body copy and several subheads, the most economical method of assembly would probably be by hand, in a studio. Of course, a rough layout must be agreed and a prototype unit produced. Thereafter, most of the components can be reproduced photographically and display lines hand lettered or transfer lettered in colour. If required, other features such as slabs of colour or borders could be added by hand or transfer film.

Sometimes, trade or industrial displays are limited to just one showroom and, after a design has been approved, will be prepared by hand using either an artist or specialist contractors depending on the nature of the work and the abilities of local suppliers. In other instances, such as where a company produces goods for resale by office supply houses, the display needs may closely resemble those of the retail trade.

Whereas most retail material has a limited life, trade and technical displays can, with suitable revisions, last for several years. Patently, therefore, the additional cost of producing a first-class job will be vindicated, but do please ensure that the units are kept clean, up to date and tidy. Although these principles are apparent to anyone with a modicum of sense, it is not at all unusual to enter reception areas in which the displays are dirty, shabby or disintegrating. This is completely contrary to their purpose, so ask the receptionist to dust them daily, keep an eye on them yourself and make sure they are properly maintained.

Checklist

Retail displays

1. Have you defined the purpose of the material and where it will be used?
2. Does your copy theme reflect the message in other media?
3. Have you closely considered the ideal size, form and materials?
4. Did you consult the printer about costs before putting the design in hand?
5. Have you shown a dummy to typical retailers or agents?
6. What arrangements have you made to test the project before producing large quantities?
7. Have you asked yourself why the retailer should decide to put your piece on display?

Trade and industrial displays

1. Have you agreed a colour layout with your artist or contractor?
2. Have you consulted local studios and display contractors to find the best suppliers for the job?
3. To save money, can you use standard, portable displays?
4. Are the displays in your reception area or showroom clean, up to date and well maintained?

Chapter 18

Outdoor and Transport Advertising

To eliminate the possibility of misunderstanding at the outset, let us first list the enormous variety of sites we shall be examining in this chapter. They include: every type of hoarding; interior and exterior positions on all kinds of transport; sites at railway stations, bus shelters, airports and the like; sites on municipal property or equipment, including glass banks; sites for electric signs; panels on the facias of shops; and, indeed, any other outdoor sites for which planning permission has been granted for advertising purposes.

Reminders

Some of these sites are so expensive that clearly they are well beyond the purse of small businesses; major electric signs in central London would be a good example. Further, because repetition is a particularly important factor in this form of publicity, the budget must be based on booking a selection of sites which will be seen regularly by large numbers of people. You should note, too, that the main function of outdoor positions is often to augment advertising in other media, by reminding the public at large of a brand or company name and one outstanding feature or idea connected with it.

To clarify this assertion, let us take as an extreme example the proprietor of a small landscape gardening business who has never advertised before, except in the classified columns of local newspapers, but is persuaded to take one double crown (20 × 30in or 508 × 762mm) space on a prominent site in the middle of a busy shopping centre. On this he paints the message, 'Blogg's Gardens. Large or small. Supreme in the south. Phone xxx.'

Poor Mr Blogg has committed every possible error. Very few people know of his service and therefore the sign cannot remind; the copy is confusing, means nothing to the uninformed and might even refer, so far as they know, to a place of interest; the message is too long to be read and understood by those who pass by in cars or buses; it is neither interesting nor memorable, and will be seen so infrequently by most people that its impact will be negligible.

This misuse of a poster site illustrates the five most important rules of outdoor advertising when its purpose is to remind:

1. Be seen frequently
2. Demand attention
3. Be very brief
4. Be easy to read on the move
5. Be easy to understand.

The last point is elementary, yet often ignored. There is absolutely no point in placing your name and message before the public unless everyone clearly understands your statement and associates it with a benefit of some kind. Never allow an artist to emulate the much too clever efforts of the few national advertisers, who sometimes bask in the adulation of the marketing press for posters which no one can interpret. Companies with huge advertising appropriations can afford such eccentricities; small businesses cannot.

Posters and cards that inform

Now consider a very different kind of site, where the public have ample time to read the copy, as they do for example, in railway carriages or buses, on stations, in waiting areas or at bus stops. Here you can, if you wish, inform, explain and persuade; indeed, with captive readers who are able to study your message several times over, it might in many cases be wasteful merely to remind. Large numbers of words are not essential, but do observe that humorous or detailed illustrations, which can be scrutinised at length, may be extremely effective. You can even introduce a series of different posters or cards — similar in some ways to a press campaign — to maintain interest.

Campaign planning

From the comments so far it is apparent that outdoor and transport advertising can play two roles — to remind or inform — depending on the location of the sites, and it is important to bear this in mind when planning a campaign. 'Reminder' sites are normally used to support advertisements in the press or on radio or television. Sites which are suitable for informing may, in special circumstances, comprise the chief medium in a campaign. Thus, for London commuters who do not take a local or evening paper, tube-car panels are a useful source of information, and can be employed to reach and influence large numbers of travellers. The latter have ample time to read a long story, and the medium may for this reason be used effectively without supporting advertisements elsewhere, although backing in some form would be much preferred.

You can also select sites which in general terms will reach certain types of people. The backs of buses will be seen by motorists; interior panels will be read by children or adults who for one reason of another do not always travel by car. Posters on British Rail commuter stations will be seen by office workers and executives; overseas travellers, also including executives, can be reached at airports. Posters in shopping areas will be seen by housewives; sites in car parks will be noticed by motorists.

If, therefore, you believe that posters or transport sites can play an effective part in your advertising programme, the first step is to assemble a list of the various alternatives in the area you wish to cover, so that the merits of each can be compared. To investigate what is available from local authorities, bus companies, taxi firms, British Rail, airports, ferry terminals and poster contractors both local and national, you should consult a recent edition of *BRAD*, local and London telephone directories or similar reference works in order to trace the relevant bodies and their addresses. A letter or telephone call will bring details of suitable sites and much additional data. You will read about solus positions, sizes, special terms for booking sites in quantity or over a long period, poster specifications, the cost of changing posters more frequently than at set intervals, and much more, including the terms of business.

There will be a great deal to study, analyse and compare. Then, naturally, you must visit the sites to assess their value, taking into account busy and slack periods. The rates quoted are for space only and you must allow for the extra cost of signwriting by hand or printing the posters. Here you should note that posters are prone to damage, and in some cases may be spoiled by graffiti. The contractors usually undertake regular inspections and replacement, and you must supply extra copies accordingly. Although the replacement service is normally reliable, it is advisable to make your own inspections occasionally, and you must allow for these as well in your costings if journeys are involved.

One of the prime considerations must be the size of your posters or cards. You will see from the contractors' literature that there are some standard dimensions to choose from, but where budgets are tight you must decide on the one size that suits your intentions and your pocket best. Typical poster sizes are:

Double crown	2ft 6in × 1ft 8in	762 × 508mm
4-sheet	5ft 0in × 3ft 4in	1524 × 1016mm
16-sheet	10ft 0in × 6ft 8in	3048 × 2032mm
48-sheet	10ft 0in × 20ft 0in	3048 × 6096mm

The dimensions of exterior or interior spaces on buses, tube trains and the like vary so much that you should investigate them with care. By sensible planning it may be possible to scale artwork or trim posters or other material to fit more than one size, but advice on these local problems should be sought from contractors. Even then, you will be wise to discuss the subject with your artist and perhaps produce rough layouts in the selected dimensions before actually booking space. With a little thought at this stage it might be possible to use cards or small posters for display purposes, too, perhaps mounted on board or adapted in some way.

A matter that may need further debate is the material to be used. For exterior spaces on buses you may have the option of supplying posters which are printed on either paper or pvc. The contractors will specify the paper substance or type of pvc, but you are, nevertheless, faced with a choice and must arrive at a decision which will affect your budget. A plastic material will last very much longer than paper, but if you plan one or more changes of poster design during the campaign it might be an unnecessary expense.

Gradually, as you ponder the various opportunities and restrictions that come to light, logical decisions will be reached, at first in outline and then in concrete terms when costs are reviewed. Now is the time to contemplate the creative approach and assess the related production expenses before finally booking your sites.

Producing your posters

First, of course, you must find a theme on which your campaign will be based. If posters are used to support advertisements in the press or on radio or television, the copy will spring automatically from the fundamental message they convey. Ideas, slogans, illustrations or claims will merely be adapted to suit the new medium, and the process is unlikely to cause you or your artist any serious problems.

When posters or cards play an informative role, however, the copywriting and design become more difficult. Attention must be claimed in competition with surrounding people, objects and events. Humour or a light approach may help, but if you plan to use a number of sites over a long period it might be advisable to produce a series of different advertisements, to maintain interest and offer new inducements.

Take as an example a retailer who has decided to book sites in a number of local bus shelters to persuade passengers that travel is quicker, more convenient and cheaper by moped or motor scooter. He advertises regularly in the local press but realises that when passengers are waiting for buses in the cold, or are late home because of bus delays, they are likely to be attracted by the idea of low-cost, alternative transport, and advertisements on the subject will be studied with enthusiasm. He writes five headlines that will exploit these situations:

Make haste with a MOPED	(time saving)
Make free with a MOPED	(independence)
Make sense with a MOPED	(convenience)
Save with a SCOOTER	(cheaper travel)
Shop around with a SCOOTER	(easier shopping)

From this outline scheme, it will be a simple matter to compose draft copy and develop a lively presentation with the help of an artist. The slogan and design motifs used in his press advertising will be introduced to aid recognition.

From groundwork of this kind a campaign will unfold, but you should still observe the rules of advertising explained in Chapter 8 and follow the advice on how to write effective copy. Note also that when the objective of your cards or posters is to inform, it may, in the right circumstances, be sensible just to adapt your press advertisements, remembering that although you see your own publicity material time after time, day by day, the public do not see it as often and are unlikely to read your message so regularly that they lose interest. Constant repetition of the same idea is not as boring as you might believe. Even the same old joke can be enjoyed, but if you attempt a witty approach do please be quite sure that it is easy to grasp and the standard of humour is high. This applies to both words and illustrations. Avoid at all costs tasteless or vulgar notions, childish quips or remarks that might be misconstrued. On the other hand, humour that is cleverly pitched at exactly the right note can be very powerful, as campaigns in every medium, including outdoor and transport advertising, have proved over the years.

In the early stages of your creative work, as soon as elementary ideas and, perhaps, rough layouts have been produced, you should refer to the contractors' rate cards and literature to consider printing requirements. Study the subject with great thoroughness, since unforeseen snags may otherwise arise. For example, to allow for reposts, recommended quantities are often given; the type of adhesives used on pvc posters is usually defined; paper sizes and the limits imposed by frameworks on display areas may be explained. Be cautious, even to the extent of sending layouts and specifications to the contractors for vetting if in doubt. Controversial copy or illustrations, or borderline claims, should also be submitted to contractors if you have the slightest reason to think they may be rejected.

Failure to observe these simple precautions can result in your being required to reprint posters or cards at much extra expense.

When copy and design are finally agreed you can put the artwork and printing in hand in the usual way, as outlined in Chapters 12 and 13, but do ensure that the printers who quote are fully versed in the kind of work involved. It would be most unwise, for example, to expect the little silk screen shop you normally use for tickets to produce elaborate and complex 16–sheet posters. Patently you would need the services of suppliers who could present evidence of long experience in this field.

If you doubt your ability to cope with this specialised work, or you have insufficient time to handle the detail, you should consult the contractors, who may offer a production service or recommend suitable firms whom they know to be reliable. In any case, you should certainly seek the contractors' advice on production if you book an electric sign or reserve a site on which a poster is to be written by hand.

Checklist

1. Will the budget allow you to book enough sites to ensure adequate repetition in the area you must cover?
2. Have you defined the role your posters or cards will play? Will they remind or inform?
3. Will your sites be seen by the right kind of prospects?
4. Have you visited the sites to assess their value?
5. Does your budget allow generously for production costs?
6. Have you investigated poster or card sizes and materials?
7. Do the reminder posters closely support your advertisements in other media?
8. For informative purposes, can you adapt your existing press advertisements for use as cards or posters?
9. Does your copy comply with the rules of advertising?
10. Have you consulted rate cards and literature to ensure your posters or cards comply with the requirements specified?
11. Are the printers who submit quotations fully experienced in this kind of work?

Chapter 19

Radio and Television Advertising

Radio advertising

Long before the 1939–45 war commercials were reaching the UK from Radio Luxembourg. The medium cannot therefore be described as new in this country, although, of course, there was no major expansion until the 1970s when it was officially introduced. For reaching specific groups of prospects, radio advertising has very special advantages and should most certainly be considered by small businesses, when appropriate, if a realistic budget can be allocated.

First, let us consider some of the groups of listeners you are able to reach during a normal weekday:

6am to 9pm: families at breakfast; people travelling to work by car.

9am to 4pm: housewives, many of whom listen to the radio while doing their chores.

4pm onwards: people returning home from work by car; teenagers and young adults when programmes are suitable.

Obviously there are other categories, and listening habits will be completely different at weekends. Radio stations investigate such matters in depth and will supply useful facts, examples and statistics if you send for a rate card. The listening and statistical patterns will vary from region to region, depending on local industries, wealth distribution and many other factors. For instance, in rural areas the majority of people travel to work by car, but in the London suburbs vast numbers still commute by public transport; many middle-class and wealthy people live in the southern coastal region, but in most other areas there are patches of poverty. Facts of this kind will affect campaign planning and creative work.

Radio stations divide weekdays and weekends into time slots, some of which have proved more valuable than others because they reach bigger audiences. They therefore cost considerably more when booking advertising spots. It does not always follow, however, that you need to broadcast at peak times, and in some cases to do so would be positively wasteful. A small chain of music shops, selling discs, tapes, sheet music and instruments, chiefly to youngsters, would probably find inexpensive slots in a Monday to Sunday, 6pm to closedown segment, more effective.

The sales director of your local station will give you expert guidance in these matters. He or she will explain the variety of special 'packages' that every station offers: there may be discounts for prepayment or volume orders, test marketing incentives, deals to encourage local small businesses, recruitment offers and similar inducements. Rates are always lower for quantity bookings — typically for over 21, 35 or 49 spots. Often a request for transmission at specified times will be complied with wherever possible, but not guaranteed.

Newcomers to radio advertising should always run test campaigns to appraise the script, production and schedules.

Although the medium is widely regarded as essentially one that reaches the general public and is thus suitable only for advertising consumer products or services, there can be a case for using it to influence business people or recruit staff. Most executives in the provinces drive to work; many listen eagerly to news and comment of the day, both national and local. Here, then, is a chance to speak to them while they are undisturbed by telephones, questions from colleagues or the latest crisis in the office or factory. For the same reasons, recruitment advertising can be effective at this time.

When planning a radio campaign aimed very largely at drivers, you should always take into account the road hazards that may demand their concentration at intervals, thus diverting attention from your message. Remember also that drivers are unable to note addresses or telephone numbers unless they are stationary. Repetition, then, and simple devices in the script to help them recall a name or number, are the obvious answers to these problems.

In fact repetition is the true key to success in this medium. Without printed information for reference, and lacking the pictorial advantages of television, you must depend on reiteration supported where possible by a series of mental images. Strangely, image creation is an acknowledged attribute of radio broadcasting, and one which the advertiser can exploit to his great benefit.

Radio can be used both to remind and inform. Spots of ten seconds' duration are ideal for the former, but longer commercials, lasting up to a minute, will usually be needed to develop an interesting story.

The factor that distinguishes this medium from the others discussed so far in this book is its ability to entertain on a completely different plane, with music to set the mood, sound effects and male or female voices, young or old, which can be identified with a specific class and age group. An appeal to the emotions can be made through melodies, jingles, sounds and voices that create powerful, compelling pictures in even the dullest imaginations.

Preparing the campaign

For successful advertising, a logical plan of campaign that makes full use of radio's special advantages is essential. If, having assembled some information about the markets reached by a station, you intend pursuing the possibility of using it, you should most certainly consider employing an advertising agency. Failing this, you must rely on the advice and guidance of the station's sales director and his colleagues. Their prime objective will be to prove to you, a potential client, the many advantages of radio advertising. To do so they may well offer very generous incentives in the hope that, having profited from the initial campaign, you will become a regular broadcaster. After agreeing a test schedule in principle, you must then solve the question of how to produce your very first commercial. A script, complete with directions, is required and you must therefore seek an experienced writer. The radio station will, if you wish, introduce you to a suitable source or you may prefer to seek the help of an independent specialist.

Whatever your decision, the writer will need a detailed brief, including your proposed radio schedule, copies of relevant press advertisements, sales literature and other material, plus a clear statement on the purpose of your campaign and the role you believe radio advertising will play in achieving it. If you are testing the medium, you should also agree the best means of evoking a tangible response.

Eventually a draft will be ready for your comments. Do not be unduly surprised if the writer wants to adjust the length of the spots or even amend the intervals between them. From experience he will gauge the impact of the proposed commercials and should be qualified to advise on how they can be presented to best effect. If his arguments are based on sensible principles you will be prudent to accept his suggestions and make any necessary adjustments to the schedule before placing a firm order.

Now you must produce the recording itself. If the writer is a member of a production company he will supervise the work for you; otherwise he will certainly recommend someone reliable, but since the subject is so technical you should ask him to oversee the work and act as your consultant. When you hear the first tape, by all means ask questions and express any strong feelings you may have, but do try to make positive and reasonable comments. Provided the production is both rational and interesting, and you have only minor criticisms, it might be best to accept the specialists' counsel. On the other hand, of course, should it be silly, vulgar or out of sympathy with your sales policy, you must insist on immediate revisions. If you study the script carefully in the first place and question the writer closely before approving it, such misunderstandings are unlikely to arise, although the sense of almost any text can be distorted by intonation, emphasis and sound effects.

After accepting the recording, you should listen to the first broadcasts and await results. If your commercial invites a direct response you will soon be able to measure its value.

Television advertising

During the 1950s commercial television quickly demonstrated its phenomenal marketing power. Indeed, so eager were many national advertisers to cash in on this unique means of reaching and persuading mass audiences that fortunes were quickly diverted to the medium, leading to complaints that television contractors had been granted a licence to print money.

Since that early experience, the value of commercial television has been proved time and again in countless campaigns both nationally and locally. Presentation techniques, too, have advanced over the years, while the higher standards of picture definition and the introduction of colour have improved the medium's potential almost beyond comparison with those pioneering days of excitement, experiment and wonder.

Unfortunately, the high cost of television advertising puts it outside the reach of many small firms, especially in heavily populated territories where the rates are correspondingly higher. In this medium repetition is essential to success, so that although the price, say, of a ten-second spot might equal that of a 20cm by 2-column space in a local newspaper, the latter will usually be more effective than a single commercial.

You should also understand that, apart from such exceptions as the Channel Islands, television can give only blanket coverage. Thus, although your market may extend to a 10- or 15-mile radius from your headquarters, a television commercial will reach much greater distances. Clearly, the waste can be enormous, and despite the fact that some stations will give a choice of area within a region, even then that area is very large.

Contractors appreciate these problems and will mitigate them where possible with special 'packages' and discounts for new or local advertisers, new products, test marketing and the like. They also offer a variety of ancillary marketing services to support a campaign.

Preparing the campaign

Television advertising is so important to those who sell their goods or services on a national scale to the public, that the various regions are often treated as distinct marketing areas. Thus, the south might be used to test a completely new brand before seeking wider distribution. Alternatively, an improved version of an established product might be introduced in the north to assess attitudes and the degree of acceptance by regular users, before committing the company to mass production of the improved design.

The sales controller of a television company has an intimate knowledge of his territory and can cite many fruitful campaigns. His advice is invaluable if you can afford to mount a marketing programme within a selected region using television as the main platform, perhaps with advertisements in other media. You could also use the complementary resources, including research specialists, mailing houses, house-to-house distributors and spearhead sales forces — all with special local information and contacts — which have been set up specifically to help advertisers achieve distribution and sales in that region.

Television is equally valuable for boosting sales nationally or regionally, countering a competitor's activities, selling direct to the public, persuading prospects to visit a store or showroom, securing enquiries, supporting a mailing or house-to-house campaign, drawing attention to press advertisements, or even advertising to a trade or industry. In the last case, however, it is normally advisable to advertise in an appropriate slot, such as during or following a farming programme if the products are exclusively of interest to farmers or growers.

The sales controller will gladly send you his rate card and literature, from which you will soon calculate whether television advertising is likely to be within your budget. As in radio, there are many different deals and discounts to consider and, of course, you should take these into account when estimating the cost of a test campaign. If you then believe the medium may have possibilities, you should seek the opinion of a reputable advertising agency since your appropriation will certainly be high enough to justify using their services.

Television advertising demands the expertise and long experience of specialists. To be effective, it needs meticulous planning and high standards of production. A static illustration with voice-over, for example, compares so badly with the professionally created commercials that it can be justified only in exceptional circumstances.

The contractors may offer to prepare your commercial, but this is akin to seeking design and artwork from a publisher and is inadvisable for much the same reasons. They may also suggest one or more independent consultants, who would probably put together a slick, workmanlike production. Resist this suggestion, too. If you can afford a television campaign of sensible size you are in a bigger business league and must be guided by exactly the right people — able to harness the required technical knowledge, special skills and marketing experience to ensure that your allocation is spent wisely. Those people are advertising agents, who will bargain very hard on your behalf and may save you appreciable sums when booking the schedules. Do listen well to their recommendations on production. Be prepared to budget liberally for making the commercial itself, even if you must trim your costs elsewhere.

How to find and select a suitable advertising agency is discussed in Part 7.

Checklist

Radio advertising

1. Have you defined your advertising objectives and the group or groups of listeners you wish to reach?
2. Have you studied with great care the station's rate card and literature?
3. Have you investigated the possibility of appointing an advertising agency?
4. If you have decided against an agency, did you discuss your plans and ideas with the station sales director?
5. If a schedule has been agreed, did you emphasise that it is provisional until a writer has been consulted?
6. Did you study the draft script with great care? Subsequent amendments will be expensive.
7. Does the script exploit the medium's special advantages?
8. Does the script invite some form of response so that you can test its impact?

Television advertising

1. Have you defined your marketing territory?
2. Will a television campaign, in the smallest transmission area

available, give you reasonable coverage without undue waste?

3. From the rate card and contractor's literature, have you calculated the approximate cost of a test campaign?
4. Can you use ancillary services within the region, such as direct mail, house-to-house or research?
5. Will you refer to Part 7 before appointing an advertising agency?

Chapter 20

Cinema Advertising

If your product or service is likely to interest the average cinema-goer you may wish to consider using this medium either on a local scale or by ITV regions.

The audience

Cinema audiences have steadily dwindled to perhaps something over a million weekly and the largest proportion usually comprises young people, from teenagers upwards.

Here, then, is a means of advertising to an age group that might otherwise be extremely difficult to reach at low cost and on a local basis. Very few small firms can afford to advertise in the national magazines read by youngsters, and in any case such wide coverage might be inapposite, whereas the cinema gives everyone a chance to approach these very prospects in specific towns or in larger areas. For those with bigger appropriations, cinema time can be booked in the appropriate television regions to tie in with ITV campaigns, although strategy of this sort is probably beyond the means of smaller companies.

Advertising is also accepted in approximately 40 HM Services cinemas in the UK, over 30 such cinemas overseas, over 20 cinemas catering for ethnic groups in the UK, and in a number of UK holiday camps during the May to September season.

Selecting the areas

For many small businesses, cinema advertising will be used as a supporting medium in a co-ordinated campaign, but in some instances, such as a shop that specialises in teenage fashions, it could play the major part in a publicity programme. Usually the selection of cinemas is a simple task and a telephone call to the managers will establish the names and addresses of the contractors responsible for advertisement bookings. If, by chance, you are contemplating a cinema campaign on a much larger scale you should consult a recent copy of *BRAD*.

Campaign planning

From the contractors' literature you will see that advertisements can vary in duration from 15 seconds to a minute, but since there are very few other factors to be taken into account, campaign planning is straightforward.

Production methods will depend on the purpose of your advertising and the budget allocated. Television commercials on film can normally be used with little or no amendment, but as the great majority of small firms are not ITV advertisers this is no answer. Cinema contractors are aware of the problem, however, and will usually suggest a number of options. For those who plan to advertise in just one or two theatres, production costs must clearly be kept at a reasonable level in proportion to the outlay on bookings. For many types of business, therefore, contractors offer a standard message to which supplementary details are added. Provided this can be linked satisfactorily to your overall plan it may be acceptable, otherwise something more ambitious will be necessary. If your budget is modest and you are determined to test the medium, you must obviously work closely with the contractors to produce a film that reflects your campaign theme and is based on artwork supplied by your artist.

If your cash allocation for cinema advertising is substantial you should seek independent advice, and once again you will be wise to consider appointing an advertising agent.

Cinema advertising is the only medium which can provide the special benefits of colour, movement and sound at a reasonable price to small firms who advertise locally to the general public. It reaches an accurately defined area without waste, and is thus especially valuable to traders wishing to influence prospects within a small, essentially local market. Equally, it can be used to cover closely defined regions of any size up to national dimensions. Note, too, that advertisements are viewed by the greatest proportion of an audience, who will have few if any distractions to weaken the effectiveness of your message.

Checklist

1. In general, will cinema advertising reach the kind of people you wish to influence?
2. Have you listed every cinema to be used in your campaign?
3. Can standard film be linked satisfactorily to your campaign theme?

4. Before booking the schedule did you investigate the total cost of advertisement production?

Part 6

Special Techniques

Chapters 21 to 25 deal briefly with four subjects, each of which might require an entire book to cover adequately. The intention here is merely to point the way to success by explaining basic principles, highlighting the most common mistakes and misconceptions and emphasising the need for clear and simple judgements.

Chapter 21

Mail Order Advertising

Throughout a long career in advertising and marketing I have often encountered the theory that fortunes can be made by just taking bargain squares in national newspapers or magazines to sell almost any old thing.

This is completely untrue as will quickly become apparent if we ask ourselves a few elementary questions. Why on earth should readers send good money to a total stranger to buy something they have never seen? Why do people buy through the post anyway? Why should they buy the advertised product when something similar is available in the shops at about the same price? Can they trust the advertiser to send the order, and send it promptly?

Having thought about the matter in such simple terms we might be forgiven for wondering why selling direct by press advertisements has ever succeeded.

Perhaps, then, we should first define what is meant by the phrase 'mail order advertising' and consider what motivates people to shop in this way. Strictly speaking, mail order advertising refers to a form of selling in which the reader or viewer is persuaded to send cash for products which are described — and usually illustrated — in an advertisement. There are closely related forms of selling through the mail by means of literature, which can range from a single leaflet or folder to a catalogue comprising many hundreds of pages printed in full colour and offering thousands of lines. The majority of the people who buy regularly through such literature were originally enticed by advertisements to send for the catalogue or other material, but these cannot accurately be described as mail order advertisements.

People may respond to mail order because:

1. The product is unavailable elsewhere.
2. The product, or a similar one, is unavailable at that price elsewhere.
3. They live in remote districts, far from large shopping areas.
4. They have difficulty in resisting pressure from sales people.
5. They prefer to arrive at buying decisions in their own time,

at home.

6. They find certain purchases, especially intimate items, embarrassing.

Before deciding to enter this field of selling you must be absolutely sure that prospects will have at least one reason, and preferably more than one, for buying direct through your advertisements. Do not confuse their motives for buying with those of people who order through catalogues, where interest-free instalment payments and other incentives apply. Women in particular enjoy browsing through this colourful literature and will do so for hours, rather like window shopping. Your press advertisement, even if it features a number of bargains, will not have the same irresistible appeal.

A serious difficulty facing the newcomer to mail order advertising is the inability to budget realistically simply because it is impossible to forecast results. Just consider, too, the many other imponderables:

1. Can the market be accurately defined?
2. Which main medium should be used to reach it: press or television?
3. Which ITV region or which publications?
4. How long should the commercial be?
5. Or what size spaces should be booked?
6. Will colour be needed?
7. How will repetition affect the response?
8. How frequently should the advertisements appear?

Although intending advertisers will probably conclude that television is much too expensive, there are still many questions to be answered, each affecting the cash allocation and the outcome. For the inexperienced, a test campaign is the obvious solution — and one that may well prove unprofitable.

Consider, now, the reasons that traders may have for trying to sell through mail order advertisements. Commonly, a small firm is either buying a product cheaply or manufacturing at a competitive price, but is unable or unwilling to distribute through retail channels. A firm may have large stocks that are slow moving or stationary. Alternatively, a private individual may try to set up his own business by selling through the post. In my experience, these and similar circumstances are not usually conducive to success, although there are exceptions. But generally speaking, if retailers who enjoy close contact with the public's preferences and attitudes are unwilling to buy certain lines, you cannot logically expect to sell them by mail order.

Your chances of success are much increased if you are offering not just one product but a range of lines which have a sensible purpose and are likely to sell through the post because they meet one or more of the six requirements explained earlier in the chapter. If all the lines fall within one special category, such as household or DIY accessories, or they are used by enthusiasts, such as caravanners or aquarists, so much the better.

For a person who already runs a sound business and has several mail order lines to offer, the likelihood of profitable trading is again improved since even when the response is poor each customer can be sent a catalogue or list of products from which subsequent sales will be gained at negligible cost. Eventually, after dealing regularly in this fashion over a year or two, the advertiser is regarded by large numbers of readers as an established trader, and therefore trustworthy. He also builds a very valuable list of people who for one reason or another habitually buy through the post.

Unfortunately, as we have seen, developing this kind of business is more difficult than the inexperienced would believe. But for those who, despite the warnings, are determined to test its potential, the following guidelines may prove useful.

Investigation

Having decided that a product — or better still a range of products — can be sold by mail order, the first sensible step is to search through the publications which normally carry such advertisements to find similar lines and compare performance, prices and other relevant details. This will be a simple task if the market is well defined and can be approached through just a few specialised journals, such as those read by radio enthusiasts, anglers or bird-fanciers. In other cases, where subjects, such as motoring or gardening, have a wider appeal the research must embrace not only appropriate magazines but also newspapers and periodicals of a more general nature, which sometimes carry mail order advertisements for the kind of products in question.

Finally, if the lines are of common interest, the search must be correspondingly widespread, bearing in mind, of course, price ranges and hence the sort of publication in which they are likely to be advertised.

Cut out specimens of every advertisement you find, note on it the publication and date, and build a file which can be extended as your research progresses.

From the information gathered you will have a fair picture of the market in which you are interested. Look particularly for advertisers who are very active, and order goods from them to study not only the products themselves but also the accompanying literature. Note how quickly you receive the goods and how they are packed. From *BRAD* or other sources calculate the costs of every advertisement and try to assess how many sales will be needed to cover the total expenses, including postage.

After assembling so much intelligence and attempting a number of costings you must reach a decision for or against a test campaign, and whether to employ an advertising agency.

Let me at once advise you against running your own programme, for in truth this is a specialised field in which long experience pays dividends. If you can find advertising agents with the right background, they may even have undertaken a similar project in the same market and thus be able to give you much invaluable counsel. They could perhaps save you money by warning against the scheme, or recommending a plan that would eliminate fruitless experiment.

Nevertheless, there are examples of companies which have developed a flair for successful mail order advertising without professional help, and for the benefit of readers who believe they can follow those adventurous footsteps I would offer some rudimentary principles.

Media planning

The nature of the product or products to be advertised will often point to the most suitable publications. If you are selling to a comparatively small and well-defined market served by just one or two journals, study several issues of each to determine the tactics used by regular, well-established mail order traders: note the sizes of their advertisements, the frequency of insertion and the positions they occupy. Although you will wish to devise your own, logical plan of campaign and will, quite rightly, eschew copy-cat policies, it would be imprudent to ignore certain lessons completely.

If, for example, quarter-page spaces are used regularly to sell products which in some respects are similar to your own, it might be rash to book full pages when the copy can reasonably be condensed to fit a smaller space.

Products with a wider appeal will present greater problems which are usually best solved by playing safe whenever possible. For example, although a great number of newspapers and magazines carry gardening features, which are often surrounded by advertisements, many inviting direct orders, it would be advisable to use the gardening weeklies at the outset to test both copy and media. In this way you are reaching readers who are enthusiastic enough about the subject to buy special publications and are therefore better prospects. Of course, as soon as your advertisements appear you will be bombarded by literature and telephone calls from optimistic advertisement managers and space salesman representing every conceivable publication that carries a gardening feature. Refuse their offers politely but firmly until the results of your test can be analysed. When you have proved the value of specific publications and are trading profitably, with copy that works efficiently, experiments in other newspapers or periodicals will be warranted.

The greatest problems of all are presented by products with universal appeal, since they must usually be tested in publications which are read by a suitable cross-section of the public. Moreover, my experience has shown that local and regional magazines or newspapers rarely pull sufficient orders to cover costs, presumably because they lack the prestige and punch of the nationals. One must therefore use the latter, which are expensive. Sometimes, to reduce the outlay, a test can be restricted to the regional editions of certain widely read publications such as *Radio Times* or *TV Times*.

Many beginners point to the bargain squares in popular magazines and the weekend newspapers, believing that by some strange magic they will attract business on an enormous scale. Undoubtedly some regular advertisers trade profitably from these squares, but you will find that the goods on offer fall into special categories such as domestic or handyman devices, many being unobtainable elsewhere. Before committing yourself to the medium, do study the lines that seem to be good sellers carefully and decide whether yours are comparable.

After compiling the list of publications to be used you must decide how many insertions will appear in each, the optimum intervals between insertions and the ideal timing. A novice is often tempted to test the pulling power of just one advertisement in each publication — a plan to be resisted with great determination. Repetition, as we have seen, leads first to recognition and then to confidence. Three insertions would be the very minimum; better by far to reduce the number of publications on your schedule than lose the advantages of a series. Furthermore, intervals between insertions should be brief in order to gain the benefits of being recognised and trusted.

If your advertisements are to appear in monthly magazines, decisions about timing will not usually be difficult although seasonal demand must be taken into account. Obviously, however, weekly publications require deeper thought since the choice of dates is so much wider. For example, you should ask yourself whether readers are more likely to buy at the end of a month when a salary cheque has arrived in the bank; would it be better to run a series of advertisements for Christmas gifts in November or December or split the insertions between each month? Should they appear weekly or fortnightly?

Clearly, then, the insertion dates in daily publications will demand even deeper thought. An advertising executive who specialised in mail order once advised me that Monday is the premium day for direct response advertising. This claim I have never believed and never understood, preferring the theory that readers are more inclined to respond during their leisure time at weekends. But there are no rules to follow on this subject; be guided by the nature of your product and your own common sense.

Having read this chapter so far, you may now find it helpful to return to Chapters 5 and 6 on media planning and space buying since the principles they expound apply equally to mail order programmes.

At this stage you will be wondering why there is no reference to either the Sunday newspaper supplements which carry so much mail order advertising, or to the direct response commercials on ITV. These omissions are deliberate simply because the cost of participation is so high that you should seek the services of an advertising agency to reduce the risk of failure. This is no territory for beginners.

Reader protection schemes

Before we leave the subject of media, however, I must mention the reader protection schemes run by national newspapers, magazines and most other publications. Before bookings for mail order advertisements can be accepted, you will be required to complete a detailed questionnaire which seeks much confidential information on your products, stocks and your business standing. You may also be required to contribute towards an insurance fund. As arrangements and conditions could vary in the future they are not summarised here. Current literature will be supplied by the publishers on request, and because there may be some delay in accepting your application, you should send for details early. Note, too, that the schemes differ in some particulars if not in intent and you should apply separately to newspapers and magazines for the information you seek.

Many would-be advertisers object to answering the questionnaire and contributing to the funds, but you should appreciate that the schemes are intended not only for reader protection but also to increase confidence in mail order advertising itself. Unless you co-operate fully your space bookings will not be accepted, and there is no way of avoiding the formalities. You must also, of course, arrange refunds for any customers who, because they are dissatisfied, return your goods soon after purchase.

Producing mail order advertisements

Naturally the advice in Chapters 7 to 10 is still valid, but because you are seeking an immediate response, every word, every feature must be selected or designed to that end. Your advertisement replaces the shop window, the showroom, the display and the salesman. Just as a passer-by is enticed by something on show in a window and enters the store to examine it, so must your advertisement gain attention and arouse so much interest that a purchase is seriously considered.

Then, just as the salesman emphasises the product's special benefits and firmly closes the sale, your advertisement must be equally positive. In fact, the most important advantages should be highlighted twice or more by illustration or repetition, and the exhortation to buy must be repeated by suggestion and direct statement.

Examine closely the very best mail order advertisements and learn from the examples they set. Note that in many cases the act of buying is made so very simple, sometimes by just telephoning and quoting a credit card number. See how attention is gained by unusual or imaginative headlines. Read the copy and notice how easy it is to understand; mark the use of short, powerful words, perhaps evoking mental images that compel interest and create desire. Note, too, that the illustrations are uncluttered, and that where space allows they include an interesting person, or present products in an ideal setting, both of which readers can identify with. Observe the strong encouragement to buy immediately.

Now study the smaller mail order advertisements and bargain squares. See how brief descriptions and elementary line drawings are used to convey a great deal of information within tiny areas.

Note that mail order copy is essentially factual, even in the larger spaces. A fanciful headline, followed by a brief introduction, may be used to attract the eye and set the mood. Thereafter, the reader is bombarded with benefits and descriptions, and where space permits a coupon is included. When there is a choice of style, colour and size, a coupon becomes essential to reduce the risk of error, confusion or disappointment, thus cutting the expense of replacing unsuitable merchandise or, worse still, sending refunds.

When discussing the design and artwork for a mail order advertisement with your artist, you should insist that the layout is kept simple, display type and body matter are very easy to read and the various elements are presented in a logical selling order, preferably with at least one bold feature that directs the reader's eye to the coupon or the exhortation to order. The illustration, also, must be simple, clear and easy to interpret; a small half-tone, for example, might reproduce badly on newsprint and a line drawing would therefore be safer.

To assess the performance of both copy and media, keep an accurate tally of the results from each advertisement in every publication. The procedure will be simplified if you insert a reference key in coupons or in your address line. In the latter you could perhaps add fictitious room numbers or department initials. An analysis of your test campaign will provide cost-per-sale figures on which future programmes can be based.

If you are a retailer selling a number of lines at keen prices or offering unusual merchandise in mail order advertisements, you can reasonably expect callers from outside your district. This is especially likely if you sell to enthusiasts. Identifying these new customers and relating the value of their purchases will be almost impossible, but do watch for the signs, such as clipped advertisements or casual remarks, that will help you recognise them.

In my experience, retailers who buy shrewdly and treat their mail order activities as subsidiary business, may gain substantially from the additional source of income that such advertising can produce. In the next chapter we will examine the other forms of advertising which can accelerate retail turnover.

Checklist

1. Is your merchandise, at the proposed price, suitable for selling by mail order?
2. Have you examined mail order advertisements for similar products? How do the latter compare with your lines?
3. Have you ordered specimens of these products for study?
4. Have you investigated, in great detail, every publication that may be suitable?
5. Have you planned to book at least three insertions in each

publication?
6. Have you given careful thought to timing and the intervals between advertisements?
7. Have you asked the publications for details of their reader protection schemes?
8. Is your advertisement copy, including headlines, text and illustrations, designed to encourage immediate response?
9. Have you in one form or another repeated the main selling points and exhortations?
10. If there is room, have you remembered to include a coupon?
11. Have you made the act of ordering as simple as possible?

Chapter 22

Advertising a Shop or Store

Mail order activities excepted, the sole reason for retail advertising is to entice prospects into the shop. In general, this can be achieved by announcing special bargain prices, or by claiming that you sell goods which are unobtainable elsewhere in the district, or simply declaring that you sell specific kinds of merchandise of a certain grade or quality. Of these techniques, the first suggests an aggressive policy, while the second approach is in many ways equally powerful since in essence you are saying, 'Buy it here to save travelling miles for the same thing.' Although the third technique seems much the weakest, this is not necessarily so if you sell very expensive or special products or you serve the top sector of a market. Indeed, to adopt a more thrusting manner in some circumstances might be harmful.

Positioning your business in the market

Unhappily, such elementary principles are not always understood, as a glance through any local newspaper or periodical will prove. The delicatessen, which has so many exciting foodstuffs and flavours to choose from, merely presents a list of provisions in the dullest of layouts when it could so easily describe delectable meals or snacks unobtainable from ordinary grocers in town. The butcher whose customers are mainly of the lower middle class, describes himself as a 'purveyor of meat and poultry' when, to counter the competition from a nearby supermarket, he should be aggressively emphasising the benefits of buying from a 'real butcher'.

Inexplicably, even the most highly regarded shops are allowed by custom to run one or two sales every year, although to overstep the mark and run three might be seen as positively vulgar.

Manifestly, the retailer's advertising methods must in some cases be guided by tradition and reflect his or her trading policy, but once the style has been set he will be unwise to depart from it except, perhaps, in a sale when price inducements will not offend.

Every shop or store can have its own special attractions and personality, deliberately developed and publicised to give it a singular position in the district. For shoppers, price is not always the prime consideration: not everyone will queue at a checkout to save a penny or two; most people appreciate and prefer skilled advice when buying, say, tools or furnishing fabrics; many housewives can be tempted to switch to the local bakery for their bread in preference to the sliced and wrapped mysteries sold by many of the chains.

For a small retailer who must fight the slashed prices and ruthless tactics of local self-service stores, the right kind of advertising will help to establish a reputation for courtesy and standards of attention to the needs of individual customers that the large competitors just cannot match. Note, however, that advertising by itself will not usually bring potential customers hot-foot to your premises. Shopping habits, developed over many months or years, are difficult to break; most people are happier to patronise stores they know, while housewives will even follow the same route, week after week, buying from familiar assistants in familiar shops.

It is apparent, therefore, that in order to invade the prospect's routine your advertising must offer something very special. An exciting message in the press will not normally be sufficient unless you are presenting truly amazing bargains or introducing something new and incredibly interesting. Nevertheless, an unusual advertisement will at least start the weaning process, which will be hastened by supporting messages in other media such as house-to-house circulars, posters or cinema advertising.

Window displays

A critical time arrives when the prospect is close to your premises, since this is the very moment at which a long habit may be broken. Logically, your windows must display bold reminders that form a link with your advertisements. This elementary principle, so manifest, so easy to implement, is seldom observed. The link can be as simple as enlarged versions of current press advertisements, posters from a local campaign or just a slogan or catch-line, presented, perhaps, on a showcard or banner.

But a link should not stop at the windows. Inside, adjoining the relevant goods or in other strategic positions, appropriate reminders will reap even greater advantage from your advertising. Price tickets, for example, might carry a pertinent message; a showcard or sticker near the till will once again remind and encourage.

Quite apart from these campaign tactics, advertising can play a vital part in a retailing policy which seeks good returns from very low margins coupled with rapid turnover. Of course, a small business will find it hard to compete in every respect with the large chains, but by astute buying and rejecting the temptation to take traditional margins, the retailer may build a trading position for himself which can be exploited to great advantage by the right kind of publicity. Understandably, it takes courage to sell with so little return per unit and perhaps even more to slash the prices of slow-moving lines to release money for new purchases. However, such methods do produce fascinating opportunities for creating lively, eye-stopping advertisements, which in turn reinforce the retailer's reputation for keen trading.

Of course, the principles of campaign planning and advertisement production described in earlier chapters still apply, although special purchases and price reductions will inevitably require an unusual degree of flexibility. Recognition can best be ensured by introducing common features, such as standard borders, name styles, slogans and typefaces in every form of advertising. Last-minute announcements can perhaps be catered for by the use of 'stop press' or 'bargain of the week' panels. But because the majority of advertisements for shops and stores in every medium are unimaginative, the proprietor with unusual retailing techniques and the publicity ideas to match will inevitably catch the public's attention, admiration and support.

The most important advertising medium for almost every shopkeeper, and particularly those in city centres with so many casual shoppers, is the window: it can invite, excite, advise, encourage or entice; but it can also warn off, offend or deter. So learn a lesson from the large stores, who employ teams of display specialists and spend very considerable sums on keeping their windows beautifully dressed and immaculate throughout the year. Follow this example in order to convince strangers and regular customers alike of your high standards. Every window tells a tale; be sure that yours is a happy one.

Checklist

1. Does your advertising theme truly reflect your trading policies?
2. Are you countering the activities of nearby chain stores or supermarkets by offering benefits they cannot match?
3. Are you using your advertising to help build an attractive and distinctive personality for your business?
4. In every medium, are your advertisements immediately recognisable as members of a 'family'?

5. Are your windows immaculate and do they link with your current advertising theme?
6. Have you extended this link to displays inside your shop or store?

Chapter 23

Industrial and Trade Advertising

To prevent misunderstanding, I think we should first define our subject: every kind of advertising conducted by those firms which sell their goods or services to other businesses or institutions. Of course, some concerns, such as office-supply houses or van-hire companies, trade with both the general public and many different establishments, but in this chapter we shall examine the advertising addressed only to the latter.

Concentrate your advertising

The first essential task in planning a campaign directed at one or more trades or industries, is to define the markets as precisely as possible. Sometimes the answers are obvious and the targets can be described and reached with great accuracy at reasonable cost. In other cases, however, the product or service will interest such a great variety of potential customers in so many fields, that devising a logical advertising programme is difficult, especially with a modest budget.

Usually there is a temptation to dilute a campaign's effectiveness by spreading the advertising activities far too widely, whereas the wiser plan might be to select groups or categories and concentrate the effort on just one or two at a time. In principle it is better to saturate small but important sectors of a market than attempt to cover the whole so thinly that a reasonable degree of impact and repetition cannot be achieved.

Consider, then, these contrasting examples. A company that produces a new, low-cost ticket machine for use by bus conductors, can describe its UK market with great precision as every organisation that runs a bus service and issues tickets to passengers. These prospects can be reached efficiently, quickly and regularly by direct mail advertising, perhaps supported by a press campaign in trade journals.

On the other hand, a company that distributes an imported miniature computer for business use can only define its market as every firm or institution, large or small, that will benefit from employing the equipment, either as a main computing source or as a subsidiary instrument, perhaps installed as a minor station connected to a much larger central computer.

In these circumstances, to make a small budget work beneficially, it would be prudent to select certain trades, industries or areas of commerce in which computing would give very special advantages in terms of greater profits gained by time or work saved. Thus, for selling the computer to smaller firms it might be possible to stimulate interest with 'off the peg' programs suitable for, say, estate agents or garage stores. For selling to bigger concerns, it could possibly pay to select those with several branches, such as retail chains or builders' merchants, and suggest that, since the computer is compatible with most other systems, it can be used both for internal records at branches and linking to the master instrument at head office.

Thus, test campaigns to small and much larger businesses could be conducted on a reasonable scale in appropriate trade journals, supported by direct mail advertising and participation in suitable exhibitions. Spending the same budget on more general advertisements in financial and business journals would be very much weaker in its effect since the message would be less specific.

Encourage action

Having defined the market or market sectors to be reached, the next, equally essential step is to decide exactly what action you want prospects to take. For businesses which advertise to the general public the objective is usually obvious and simple, such as visit my shop, hire my taxi or ring me to discuss home improvements. But for those who must deal with other firms or large institutions the selling process is often more complex. You may, for example, be seeking regular business on a large scale from just a few clients, in which case you could decide to impress them in the first instance by sending an elaborate brochure with a request for a meeting. You may need a constant stream of enquiries for representatives to follow up. You may be introducing a completely new production method or system and will therefore offer to send a technical paper. You may have been granted an official approval — perhaps certifying that your instrument is safe in hazardous areas — and therefore want engineers to send for your new data sheet. You may intend running an advertising campaign to the general public and be inviting retailers or wholesalers to order in advance.

We have seen in previous chapters the value of telling prospects exactly what you want them to do. In trade and industrial advertising this elementary rule, often overlooked, is just as essential. Busy executives have no time to interpret your message, so tell them clearly what action to take, and make that action as easy as possible.

Presentation

In the early stages of setting up a small business it may not be possible to allocate a sum for the year's advertising. Of course, the sensible beginner prepares an estimate of revenue and expenditure, but without previous experience to guide him the figures can be no more than an intelligent guess. For this reason he will hesitate to spend comparatively large amounts on a preliminary campaign, but he should remember the encouraging assertion in Chapter 15 on direct mail that, with a well-designed letterhead printed on good paper, matching envelopes, a typewriter and a sheet of postage stamps, anyone can become an advertiser. Here is a medium which can place your name and message on the desks of important potential customers overnight. So read that chapter once more and apply the principles to your own particular problems.

Direct mail lets you assess opinions and attitudes at negligible cost. It can help you arrange meetings with exactly the right people, or encourage them to test your product or service without your incurring the expenses of artwork or printing other than for good stationery. When it is used thoughtfully, with a logical plan of campaign and crisp, interesting copy, the medium can help to build that initial momentum so essential to every young business.

But I must stress once more the importance of doing the job properly. No one in today's world of fierce competition will heed badly composed letters presented on cheaply produced headings. So use a competent designer for your stationery, spend generously on printing, devise a series of letters that demand attention and then ensure they are faultlessly typed in every detail.

This matter of presentation is generally treated with so much indifference by smaller firms in trade and technical circles that those who take the trouble to produce attractive and interesting advertisements will certainly be noticed. Look through any industrial journal to see how the larger companies, served by their agencies, present themselves well, in the best positions. Turn, then, to the back pages and judge for yourself the lamentable standards of copywriting, illustration, design and production emanating from the minnow concerns. One wonders why they fail to realise that such advertisements are wasted opportunities — and may even be positively harmful.

Similarly, their literature and other forms of advertising are often unimaginative and poorly printed — sometimes employing the styles of the 1950s and 60s to introduce products for tomorrow's technologies. Surely they must understand that this is absurd. Sometimes, too, the proprietors of these small firms refuse to acknowledge the role of advertising in modern markets, preferring to believe that technical excellence allied to skilled manufacturing removes the need for publicity in any form, apart from a boring exposition of the product's features in a leaflet printed in one colour on inferior paper. The strength of conviction seems to increase in direct ratio to the complexity of the product.

Snobbery of this kind has no place in today's scramble for sales, when success depends on gaining interest and trust in competition with so many determined rivals.

Monitoring response

The purpose of a very large proportion of industrial and trade advertising is chiefly to feed the sales director with enquiries. It would therefore seem easy to evaluate the pulling power of the various journals on a press schedule by monitoring the replies received in the post and by telephone. Take notice, however, of the factors mentioned in Chapter 10 on copy and media testing before reaching conclusions.

Many industrial advertisers are constantly seeking ways of reducing the cost per enquiry by comparing the results obtained from different copy styles in spaces of various sizes in a number of journals. Such studies are valuable and can increase the effectiveness of your advertising, but do look for intangibles which may affect the results and remember also that accurate analysis is impossible.

Checklist

1. Can you define your markets accurately?
2. Can you avoid diluting your budget by aiming your campaign at specific groups or categories?
3. What action do you want prospects to take in your favour?
4. Can direct mail be used to reach important prospects effectively at low cost?
5. If so, have you read Chapter 15 once more?
6. Is your stationery well designed and printed on good-quality paper?

7. Do your advertisements compare well with the best advertisements in the journals on your schedule?
8. What arrangements have you made to monitor enquiries?

Chapter 24

Financial Advertising

Turn to the financial pages of any of the more serious national newspapers, particularly those which deal with family savings and investment matters in the weekend issues, and study the many different advertisements placed by companies large and small. As you examine them ask yourself whether you would entrust the originators with just a small sum of money. If your verdict is 'no' or 'doubtful', the advertisement will probably fail, since its first objective must surely be to build credibility and trust.

For the famous clearing banks and merchant bankers this question of credence presents few problems because everyone appreciates the safeguards which exist to protect their clients — and the government's interest in a healthy banking system. Equally, the reputations of the leading life assurance houses and building societies generate great confidence, although for extra safety savers will spread their capital over several of these institutions.

This policy of extreme prudence teaches small firms, such as brokers and investment advisers, an important lesson in that whereas existing clients may trust the principal's advice and judgement, and from experience believe him to be honest, his advertisements cannot possibly create a comparable degree of confidence. Therefore, in every advertising medium he must seek to convince, reassure and build an exceptional relationship.

This reasoning is so elementary that one would expect every intelligent person who runs a small business in the field of finance and investment to observe and follow the principles almost by instinct. But surprisingly, this is not always so. Return to your study of the national press and you will recognise the smaller firms at a glance by the weak copy in their advertisements and the lack of professional design. Even their claims, which surely must be true in every particular, are sometimes so poorly presented that confidence may be extinguished rather than strengthened. Here, then, are some pointers to more effective advertisements:

1. Avoid making extravagant claims, however true, unless you can reassure the reader.

2. Build confidence by choosing your words with great care.
3. Offer, if you can, a personal service of some kind which larger concerns cannot match.
4. Introduce factors which create trust, such as the year you were established or membership of a professional body.
5. Find a headline that echoes these principles. For 'Fantastic savings on car insurance' substitute 'Five times out of ten we save motorists money'. For 'Astounding investment' substitute 'Double your money in seven years — GUARANTEED by major life assurance company'.
6. Support your claims with true figures and examples when you can.
7. Build recognition and extra confidence by repeating your advertisements several times in succeeding issues of the same publication.
8. Establish an approach and style that are easy to recognise.
9. Experienced investors will criticise examples that take the best results from carefully chosen periods. Avoid falling foul of such judgements by quoting various periods, even the less favourable.
10. Use a skilled and experienced designer for every advertisement and every item of literature and stationery that reaches the public, so that you are seen to be a professional.
11. Although design and colours should be suitably restrained, try to develop a style of copywriting that conveys exciting ideas in an acceptable fashion.
12. If permitted by your professional body, a regular, free newsletter for clients and potential clients who have replied to advertisements or called at your office, is an excellent means of building confidence.

Media selection

There can be little doubt that the serious national dailies and Sunday newspapers or suitable national magazines, will in many cases prove to be the most effective press media for developing a large volume of business and will usually pull enquiries at the lowest cost. But for the majority of small firms with a purely local clientele, the publications would be entirely inappropriate. Nevertheless, the principle is clear: always seek the newspapers or periodicals which offer the greatest degree of prestige. In practice, this will often mean buying space in regional dailies or Sundays with comparatively large circulations, and in the best local magazines published for business people or wealthier members of the public. Local weekly newspapers will also justify a test campaign, but from experience I would expect the cost per enquiry to be higher.

Direct mail advertising to local businesses and business people should also be considered, particularly for special insurances and pension contracts or to prepare prospects for telephone canvassing. Lists can be built from local directories and by keeping records of visitors to your office or exhibition stands. The most valuable list, however, is your existing customers, who should receive not only regular mailings but extra literature enclosed with accounts or renewal notices.

You would expect these sales tactics to be obvious and thus unworthy of mention. In reply, I can only say that during the many years in which I have used a certain insurance broker, not once have I received a mailing of any kind, nor has literature been enclosed with renewal requests. In consequence, some of my business has been placed elsewhere.

Apart from the opportunities presented by direct mail, it might be worth testing house-to-house circulars in selected areas. I would not expect substantial results from this source, but much would depend on the nature of the contracts sought and the purpose of the campaign. If, for instance, an insurance broker were prepared to take a long-term view it might be sensible to circularise estates of 'starter' homes, seeking initially to attract small insurances — perhaps car or house contents — and hoping to build life assurance, pension or investment business later on.

It might also pay to participate in local exhibitions, or even organise your own shows in suitable hotels, possibly seeking the co-operation of insurance companies or other financial institutions for whom you act as a broker.

Other media, including cinema, radio, television and outdoor posters etc, are unlikely to be of value, but do watch your competitors, and firms outside your area, to see what you can learn from their activities. Never copy their ideas, for by doing so you forfeit the benefits of originality and may even lose local respect. Look instead for ways in which the principles can be adapted to your advantage and to match the character of your business.

Checklist

1. Is your copy believable, and will it build trust?
2. Can you establish a style that is easily recognisable?
3. Are you using an experienced and qualified designer for your

advertisements and stationery?

4. For press advertising, have you investigated the cost of space in regional dailies and Sundays?
5. For direct mail advertising, have you compiled a list of your existing clients and devised a campaign that includes inserting literature in renewal notices or accounts?
6. Have you investigated the opportunities arising from local exhibitions?
7. Have you considered organising your own shows in local hotels?
8. Would house-to-house circulars be worth testing in your district?

Part 7

Advertising Agents and Consultants

Chapter 25

The Functions and Value of an Advertising Agent

There are so many mistaken ideas about the purpose and functions of advertising agents that I must first explain their role and value in modern marketing.

During the nineteenth century agents merely accepted orders for advertisement space and passed the business direct to publishers, who allowed them a commission for recommending their publications to advertisers. Gradually the notion of helping clients devise and produce their advertisements evolved, until eventually 'full service' agencies came into being. After the 1914–18 war agency service became more sophisticated, and by the 1950s there were agencies in all the major UK cities, able to give professional advice on every facet of marketing, from press or television campaigns to public relations or research, all closely co-ordinated with the client's own efforts at market development and penetration.

Today, large agencies which serve national and international clients may employ hundreds of people in a variety of departments that might include: media buying; print buying; art; copy; press and print production; television and radio production; outdoor; accounts; voucher; marketing; research and PR. Contact with clients is maintained by account directors or account executives, and work in progress may be supervised by a traffic department. The large agencies operate in different ways, depending on their accounts and the preferences of the directors. In some cases there are two or more groups, each functioning independently, but in others certain services are centralised. Thus, for example, a creative group might comprise a visualiser, a copy chief and their assistants, all working on specific accounts, but in the same agency there might be a central department for space buying and outdoor advertising.

So far we have seen how the big agencies were developed to serve clients with massive publicity and marketing budgets. But in parallel, the medium and smaller agencies came into being to meet the needs of every kind of company, whatever its size or market — consumer, trade or technical. These smaller agencies employ a number of specialists to suit the main needs of their clients, but must rely on independent suppliers for other services. For instance, two directors might be responsible for client liaison, a third would supervise creative work, and the staff might include a copywriter, designers, a space and time buyer, a press and print production team, and a voucher and accounts department. For other functions, such as PR or television and radio production, the agency would use outside sources.

Finally, there are many kinds of advertising consultants and very small agencies, run by just two or three partners or a principal and his or her secretary. They may be well qualified by long experience and examination, and are often the ideal advisers for small firms. Unhappily, there are also a number of 'agencies' whose proprietors are completely untrained apart, perhaps, from brief employment as artists or juniors in companies vaguely connected with the advertising business. Usually such 'agencies' quickly disintegrate, but in the meantime their clients may be seriously misled by unprofessional advice.

Services offered

To understand the benefits of employing an agency we should examine the services it offers and the costs involved. First, a senior representative — normally a director — will call to discuss every aspect of your company: its history; policies; production methods; existing and potential markets; your ambitions and expansion plans; previous advertising and much more. He will talk about sales figures, turnover, margins and the effects of expansion on profits. Then he will want to discuss your immediate sales target and the budget allocated to achieve it.

After this initial meeting he will usually prepare a preliminary report and recommendations in conjunction with his colleagues. When these proposals are approved in principle by the client, he will submit an outline programme including media schedules, creative proposals and a budget. This comprehensive plan will be implemented as soon as the client agrees every detail. The agency will then order space or time, submit visuals, scripts and copy for comments and sanction, and prepare artwork and adapt it. It will then produce final material for publishers or broadcasters, obtain competitive quotations for literature, agree specifications, coordinate all these activities and ensure that delivery dates are met. The next step is to check and pay invoices for space, time and production and send invoices in summary form with vouchers to the client, who settles only one monthly statement. In addition, the agency will liaise with the client's PR consultants if required to do so, and supply much valuable information on the market, carrying out research when necessary.

Apart from this very considerable aid, the client gains all the advantages of a completely impartial opinion on his marketing strategy, plus advice and encouragement from a business confidant whose knowledge and experience of many trades and industries may prove to be priceless. Remember, too, that a good agent wants — and will help — the client's business to expand, since this will lead to bigger advertising budgets in the years ahead.

Do you need an advertising agent?

Provided you find the right agent or consultant, there can be little doubt that his expertise will make a telling contribution to the development of your business, especially if you sell in a difficult market. The services provided will also save you a great deal of work, your advertising will be much improved and your reputation enhanced.

In addition, your ability to react quickly to unfavourable circumstances, or exploit a situation to your special advantage by fast action, becomes practicable. If, for example, there is a strong possibility of your product being confused with another which has been proved dangerous, an agency can prepare an advertisement in a matter of hours to disclaim connection with the offending brand; it may also have sufficient influence with publishers to ensure the advertisement's immediate appearance. With so many other things to do, the client might find it difficult to work at this speed.

Similarly, however firm his intentions, the proprietor or marketing director is sometimes so overwhelmed by other duties that the effectiveness of an advertising campaign is diminished by delay or insufficient attention. Commonly, space is booked, but the advertisements themselves are rushed into being at the last moment, and are thus badly produced.

Furthermore, an agent may have long experience in your particular market. He may even be conversant with your product or something very similar. His value and contribution to your sucess may be considerable for this reason alone. Note, however, that an agency will not normally accept a new account if the products or services are in direct competition with those of an existing client, although this principle is not sacrosanct when an agency specialises in certain fields.

Can you afford to appoint an agency?

Provided it is recognised by the appropriate bodies, an agency is remunerated in part by the commissions received from the media, who usually allow 10 or 15 per cent on the net cost after series or other discounts have been deducted from the gross rate. This income seldom covers an agency's expenses, and nowadays the commissions are in many cases passed to the client, and a fee of 17.65 per cent is added to the net cost so that in effect the agency earns the equivalent of 15 per cent on all bookings.

In addition, the agency will probably add 20 per cent or more to everything it buys for the client, such as artwork, printing or photography. Quotations are normally submitted for special projects, including research or PR programmes.

Note, however, that an agency bargains hard on the client's behalf, and because it places so much business with the media and its main suppliers, it can often buy very keenly. The benefits of such bargaining are passed to the client, so that in many ways an efficient agency helps to pay for part of its fees. Of course, you can always find lower prices from other sources, but do understand first that an agency will normally deal only with suppliers who maintain high standards, and second that the agency attends to much of the detailed work which you, the client, must otherwise undertake.

Apart from the charges described so far, agencies may require an annual fee, depending on the nature of the product and its market, the budget and the amount of work needed to handle an account satisfactorily.

Fees and charges are always quoted and agreed before an agency is appointed. You should appreciate that just as you seek a reasonable profit from your own business operation, it is equally essential for an agency to survive and prosper. A staff of well-paid specialists is employed, and the service is expensive to provide in terms of man-hours, travelling, additional expenses and capital invested.

From previous chapters, you know that the proprietor of a small firm is quite capable of planning and implementing his own advertising programme. Indeed, instruction in the techniques involved is the very purpose of this book. Eventually, however, when a company has expanded to such a size that the proprietor or directors are under very considerable pressures from many quarters and, most important of all, the profits so justify, it will be sensible to weigh the advantages of employing advertising agents. But clearly a decision cannot be reached without careful investigation. The following chapter offers some guidelines on the procedures to adopt.

Chapter 26

Finding the Right Agency

As you would expect, the general rule is that large clients appoint large agencies. Conversely, a small business, well established and beginning to grow, will usually benefit from employing either a miniature agency or a consultant. The latter operates in much the same way as a conventional agency, but may not be fully 'recognised' by the media simply because his or her turnover is not yet high enough.

Finding the right firm to meet your special needs will require careful and patient investigation.

The first step is to compile a list of candidates within a reasonable distance of your office, bearing in mind that communications are important, especially in emergencies. Using a London consultant sounds very prestigious, but if your works are 50 miles away you will most certainly appreciate the advantages of employing a local agent, when dashing to the capital by car in the rush hour to approve last-minute alterations to press advertisements or literature.

To prepare your list, consult local directories, chambers of commerce and business friends. Include every name you can find, irrespective of size, unless you are based in a city where there are major agencies which plainly must be rejected. At this stage you are probably best advised to avoid seeking references or opinions from third parties. Instead, just ring the candidates in turn and ask for the managing director. If your enquiry receives immediate and enthusiastic attention, the firm is worth considering. Describe your company briefly and give some idea of the size of your budget for the year's advertising. If interest is expressed, ask the candidate to call at your office. Allow a full morning or afternoon for your preliminary discussions.

During your meetings with the listed agencies you should seek clear and honest answers to the following questions:

1. When was the agency or consultancy formed? Is it part of a group?
2. How many directors are there?
3. Are they qualified by examination? If so, who were the

examining bodies?

4. How many staff are there, and what are their duties?
5. What accounts does the agency handle?
6. Do they compete directly or indirectly with your product or service?
7. Do any of the executives in the agency have recent experience in your market?
8. If so, which brands or names?
9. Can you see specimens of the agency's work?
10. Will the agency prepare a report and outline recommendations without obligation? Will there be a charge for this?
11. What services does the agency offer? Which of these are handled by their own staff?
12. Does the agency have a marketing department?
13. Will the agency supply a copy of its terms of business, including notes on how charges are calculated?
14. Will the agency supply the names and addresses of, say, three clients from whom references may be sought?
15. Can you visit the agency to meet the staff and see work in progress?

You will have many other questions, depending on your products or services, and markets.

From these meetings you will gather sufficient information to narrow the choice to perhaps two or three. Of course, there may be just one outstanding applicant, with exactly the right qualifications and experience, but do not underrate the importance of building a happy and lasting understanding with the executive who will be your chief contact with the agency. You will meet this person regularly, sometimes almost daily. It is essential, therefore, to establish a rapport from which both parties will gain.

Whatever your first impressions, it is advisable to visit the agency and confirm your opinion. If there are two or more firms on your short list, a visit to each will help you reach a decision.

Even if you are completely confident about getting on well with the agency's account executive, there will be times when you deal with other members of the staff. Here, during your visit, is a chance to see them working as a team and to judge how helpful they will be when circumstances demand immediate co-operation. After the introductions, ask to see some current jobs, talk about campaigns in progress and enquire about activities which relate to your own market, or about any sphere in which you are particularly interested, such as literature production, radio advertising or launching a new product. If your questions probe too deeply into the affairs of the agency's existing clients, expect your hosts to be reticent.

Try to catch the atmosphere of the agency. If telephones ring constantly and people disappear, with suitable apologies, to answer them or deal with enquiries from staff, if the office seems to throb with purposeful industry and everyone is cheerfully busy, your conclusions may be favourable. Ask yourself whether you trust these people. Do they look, speak and act like professionals? Are they able campaigners, honed and hardened by forays into a dozen difficult markets? Is the age balance right? The exuberance and imagination of youth are fine within the boundaries of experience provided by the directors and senior staff.

From these and similar observations your final selection will be made. Be deliberate and unhurried in reaching your conclusions; base your judgement on facts; look for the glib or broad statements which indicate lack of practical knowledge or understanding; and above all be sure you have chosen properly qualified people.

Agency presentations

When an agency is approached by a company with a very large advertising allocation, it may submit its recommendations and ideas in an elaborate presentation which can include marketing reports, media plans, draft copy, visuals and much other detail. On occasions a suitable fee is charged; in other cases the work may be supplied free.

Small businesses, with modest budgets, cannot expect to receive speculative copy and designs, although most agencies will submit a simple report and suggestions without charge or obligation. During the discussions with candidates on your short list, it makes good sense to ask them for written comments and outline proposals as a further means of selecting the agency best suited to your needs.

Having at last reached a decision, this is the time to take up references and make enquiries before formally appointing the agency. Now you must give them your full trust and support; do not expect miracles overnight, but on the contrary allow them a generous period to prove their worth.

Getting the best from an agency

You should understand that the directors of an agency daily receive many demands from those they serve, and that a number of jobs require urgent action just because the client is inefficient, or has put the work to one side due to other pressures or even forgotten about it. Sometimes, too, a client gives his agency an incorrect, misleading or incomplete brief, and subsequent misunderstandings require immediate steps to extricate him from the resulting predicament.

These unnecessary emergencies sour an agent's opinion of his client and, incidentally, can be very expensive. Relationships are not improved when the client queries a bill which is ridiculously high because late working was needed, special messengers were involved or there was no time to seek quotations.

Dishonesty also destroys the agent's trust: claiming that certain advertisements are not pulling, unaware that the agent has been given the true figures by publishers from their reply services; attempting to order reprints of literature direct from a printer to save a few pounds in commission; seeking advice on copy and layouts from the agency but using an independent supplier for the production; even booking space and inserting a series of advertisements, perhaps allowing the publisher to prepare artwork.

An agent is equally disturbed when one of the client's staff, who knows nothing about copy, design artwork or print, is allowed to produce sales literature or data sheets without even consulting the agency. Remember that, quite apart from his own profits, an agent wants to see a properly co-ordinated campaign supported by appropriate printed material. Amateur interference in a well-conceived programme is stupid and guaranteed to increase agency blood pressures by at least a point.

The fact is that many — probably most — clients are guilty of these and similar crimes, usually believing that money is being saved. The price in terms of damaged reputations can be high.

Here, then, are the most important lessons on how to get the best from your agency and, incidentally, reduce your costs: organise your affairs so that every brief is clear, complete and correct; whenever possible, allow plenty of time for each job; be honest and fair. If money must be saved, discuss the problem openly with your agent. From experience he can probably suggest ways of economising without damage to your campaign.

Having advocated these fundamental attitudes I can turn to the procedures likely to be adopted as soon as the agency has been appointed. Initially the account executive will ask for a meeting at which he can examine every aspect of your business: its history; your products or services; their advantages, drawbacks or failings if any; your markets; competitors; typical customers and their buying motives; channels of distribution; seasonal factors and much more.

He will want to see your past and present literature, advertisements and supporting material. Then he will ask to see your factory, or tour your offices or store, and speak to those who make your product or supply your service. Discussions with typical wholesalers or retailers will also be arranged if appropriate, and he will probably want to spend a day or more with one of your salesmen on his journeys.

He will ask about your accounts over the past few years: annual turnover figures, gross profits, expenses and the general trading pattern. Important, too, will be a breakdown of costs and profit per sale and relevant information. He will seek your opinions on the opportunities ahead and your long-term plans and aspirations, including new products or services being developed.

Your answers to these and the many other questions should be direct and honest. Agents always welcome enthusiastic clients, but do avoid boasting or making optimistic statements which are likely to mislead. If you are reluctant to disclose private information, be assured that advertising people are constantly dealing with such matters and are most unlikely to breach your confidence.

When this broad review is complete and the agent fully understands your immediate and more distant objectives, an outline campaign will be prepared by the account executive in conjunction with his colleagues. The plan will include media schedules, draft copy or scripts and visuals for advertisements, printed matter and other items. If the agency believes that preliminary research is needed before submitting its proposals, an explanation will be given together with quotations for the work.

Eventually the final recommendations and estimates for the campaign will be presented to you, usually at a meeting in the agency itself where you will be able the question the various specialists. When the plan has been approved or suitably amended, it will be implemented by the departments concerned. Orders for space, sites or time will be negotiated and booked, artwork commissioned, radio or television material produced and progress targets fixed to ensure that copy and delivery dates are met. You will receive final media schedules, proof of press advertisements and printed matter, tapes and much else for comments and approval.

Give this work priority, since delays may require expensive overtime work. Gain the respect of your agency by inspecting every job meticulously: look for spelling errors, give figures a final check and ensure that illustrations are correct. This is no time, however, to reconsider your whole strategy or demand that copy be rewritten. Keep your amendments to the very minimum and remember that every deviation from the material originally agreed, however minor, will cost you money. For example, the addition of just a word or two in a small advertisement might require a complete resetting of the body matter and increase charges by a significant amount.

Having dealt with the approvals efficiently, you will soon receive printed matter, advertisements will be published or transmitted, posters will appear and prospects will respond.

Measure this response as accurately as you can. Keep the agency informed of the number of enquiries or orders received and the apparent increase in business. When the results so justify, send your agency a letter of thanks or congratulation. Such encouragement, so rarely received, will give everyone much pleasure and spur them to greater efforts on your behalf.

After a while you will receive the invoices for media bookings, creative work and production, supported by vouchers or certificates. Check them against schedules or estimates and pay the statements promptly. If queries arise you must, of course, discuss them with the agency, but do appreciate that niggling complaints over a pound or two may cause much irritation, especially when your changes of mind were the true cause of the extra costs.

From long experience as a consultant and agent I can confirm that clients who are reasonable in all things, and helpful in giving their approvals and understanding in emergencies, derive far greater benefits in so many ways. The account is awarded special attention by everyone in the agency and enjoys priority when competing interests must be reconciled. Be mindful of this in your relations with your agent, and reap richer harvests from your advertising budgets.

Checklist

1. After reading Chapter 25, have you calculated the additional cost of an agency, and can you afford it?
2. Is your list of candidates comprehensive?
3. Have you assembled a complete list of questions to be asked at the first interviews?
4. Have you arranged to visit agencies on your short list?
5. Have you asked these agencies to submit reports and recommendations?
6. Having appointed the best candidate, are you now setting up a system that ensures your agency is briefed clearly, correctly, completely and on time?
7. Are you meticulously checking draft copy and visuals, and

passing proofs without delay or extensive revisions?
8. Are you checking the response and sending details to the agency?
9. Do you congratulate the agency when results are especially good?
10. Do you appreciate the great benefits of developing a special rapport with your agency?

Part 8

Recruitment Advertising

Part 8

Recruitment Advertising

Chapter 27

Recruitment Media

Some firms seem to specialise in employing dunderheads. Others attract lively, intelligent staff, with places to go and a determination to succeed. Of course, much depends on the nature of the business, the type of employment and salary levels, but even so the characteristics can still vary enormously between companies in the same sphere. For instance, call at estate agency 'A' to be met by a bored typist and a sleepy negotiator who says there is nothing to match your needs in the entire district. Call, then, at agency 'B' next door to be greeted enthusiastically by everyone present and assured they have at least a dozen properties to suit.

In these contrasting examples, employer 'A' has appointed unsatisfactory staff, but his neighbour 'B' found exactly the right team. Possibly the people in agency 'A' are unhappy because of weak leadership or poor conditions, but in no circumstances would conscientious employees act so boorishly.

It is not the purpose of this chapter to lecture or advise on the quality of staff recruited by small businesses. Nevertheless, we can fairly assume that example 'B' above is preferred to 'A', and that a firm which employs ambitious people is more likely to thrive.

Having recognised the virtues of this principle, the second equally apparent need when planning recruitment is to describe accurately the nature of the job and the qualifications, leanings and experience of an ideal applicant. To be sure that every important detail is included the specification should be assembled in writing.

Finding the right media

The selection of appropriate media — and eventually the preparation of advertisements — is now very much easier since we know exactly the sort of people to be reached and the kind of message most likely to interest them. If unskilled or semi-skilled staff are required, the choice of media will almost certainly be limited to local publications because there is usually a pool of suitable applicants in every neighbourhood. Even in a comparatively small district there may be scope for advertising selectively. If, for instance, the options comprise a weekly newspaper with heavy coverage of some good residential areas, a free-sheet with blanket distribution and an evening paper which covers a radius of 30 miles, the weekly might be ideal for recruiting part-time clerks, the free-sheet could perhaps be used to find labourers, and the evening, with its much wider circulation, would probably be more effective in a search for junior representatives.

Finding senior staff, especially highly qualified technicians or professionals, will obviously call for very different media, although local publications and radio should not be automatically discarded. A working population is never static or immutable: people move into an area, others have been made redundant or are actively seeking a change; some may be tempted by appropriate inducements, or they may be ready for advancement. Past attempts at tracing suitable executives or specialists locally, however unsuccessful, should not therefore deter you from trying again. There are considerable advantages to be derived from local recruitment in that removal expenses are saved and the applicant settles down quickly without the upheaval of moving house and family.

Despite these observations, advertising on a national scale is often the only solution. When technicians or professionals can be reached accurately by the conventional trade, commercial or industrial journals, the media plan is simple unless there is a shortage of people with the desired qualifications, when it may be necessary to cast the net in other waters. But before turning automatically to the quality national newspapers, it may be helpful to pin-point areas in which such specialists are widely employed — perhaps, for instance, in the Midlands or industrial suburbs of London — and book space in suitable local or regional publications.

The most difficult problems commonly arise when selecting media for recruiting sales executives, financial directors and the like who are more likely to be reached by publications with a general appeal. Usually there are appropriate specialised journals, but you may be seeking candidates with additional knowledge. Thus, it might be essential to invite applications not just from sales executives but from sales executives with long experience in the road transport industry, not only financial directors but those with an understanding of the problems encountered in property development.

Again, before turning to the quality national newspapers, debate the advantages of other publications. Clearly, our sales executive is likely to scan the road transport journals, but the ideal financial director might read any one of a dozen periodicals. This is where the job specification referred to earlier will be useful, since it is vital to understand exactly the kind of person you wish to employ. Presumably, a small firm making its way in the demanding world of property development would be operating on a modest basis, and thus seeking an ambitious younger man or woman with experience gained through employment in a larger property company. Advertisements in publications read by top-drawer financial brains in the City of London would therefore be wasted; wiser, perhaps, to test your regional dailies or Sundays and book display spaces of reasonable size. If the response proves inadequate, it might then be better to test financial or accounting weeklies before turning to the national newspapers. Note, also, that the latter two groups of publications will pull replies from readers nationwide and thus introduce the question of removals, with the resulting delays and the problems which arise if the successful candidate is found to be unsuitable after a month or two.

For seeking various kinds of unskilled or semi-skilled people you will quickly learn the powers and weaknesses of your local media. Their value for recruiting office staff can also be assessed quickly, and you may well find, for example, that your regional evening paper is the best means of seeking secretaries or typists. Timing, too, will repay your study. Is it better to advertise on Mondays or Tuesdays, when there may be fewer advertisements, or do Wednesday or Thursday bookings work more effectively? Friday is declared by some to be a bad choice, but readers do have the chance of considering your vacancy over the weekend, with more time to compose a letter of application.

Advertisement presentation

Recruitment is one of the few fields of advertising where repetition is unnecessary. Standard and distinctive features, including borders, address lines and slogans are helpful, however, because they aid recognition, enhance your reputation and reduce production costs. The subject is discussed in the following chapter.

The size of the space to be booked will obviously depend on the importance of the vacancy, the likely ease or difficulty of filling it, the job description and the length of your advertisement copy. In some cases an announcement in the classified columns will attract ample replies, but in others a 10cm by 3-column display panel or something even larger may be called for. Copywriting and presentation techniques, again discussed in the next chapter, will influence these decisions and it is therefore important to prepare accurate layouts before sending a space order.

If you employ an advertising agency, there may be an executive on the staff with experience in recruitment advertising who can help you with the task, including the creative work. You may also be approached by an agency that specialises in the subject, although usually they are interested only in firms with very large sums of money to spend each year on advertising for personnel. But even if you are helped by experts you may find the advice in the next chapter useful.

Chapter 28

Recruitment Advertisements

Even in times of high unemployment it is not always easy to attract exactly the right staff, particularly specialists in the expanding high-technology industries. Naturally, also, when firms are discarding staff they will keep the best or most highly qualified for themselves and return the remainder to the market. It thus follows that you should always assume the ideal applicants will be difficult to find, and must be attracted by an interesting deal. Wage or salary levels are important, but most applicants will weigh, too, such matters as expectations for themselves and the employer, working conditions, the attitudes of directors or colleagues and the pleasures, fun or achievements in prospect.

Recall, as well, the assertion in the previous chapter that a firm which employs ambitious staff is more likely to prosper.

Copy

Manifestly, our approach must be lively, unusual and persuasive in order to catch the attention of the pick of the readers, encourage them to study the message and inspire them to action. Now examine the 'situations vacant' columns in any publication and judge for yourself how many advertisements meet these elementary needs. Undoubtedly there will be few, and sometimes none.

On a page in a national newspaper the following headlines appeared:

Electrical/instrument engineer
Recently qualified ACAs
Shift managers
Manager: career prospects in contract furnishing
Opportunities for physicists
Marketing — kitchens and bathrooms
Sales training manager

On that page not one headline created a vivid mental picture or suggested the excitement and challenge of working in a new job. In fact the highest score I could award for attention value or interest was 5 out of 10.

Now let us examine the copy in another of these advertisements which, again, was typical. The company name, industry and location have been altered so that no offence is caused.

> **Sales Training Manager**
> **Packed Foods**
>
> XYZ Limited is part of a £1 billion plus corporation manufacturing and marketing a wide and prestigious range of food products. A recent study has placed it among the top thirty most-admired organisations in Europe.
>
> We are seeking a dynamic and experienced Sales Trainer to join our professional and well-respected team of four. The basic manuals and computer-based programmes are well established. The need now is for someone to utilise these resources to develop a sales team able to deliver results in an increasingly competitive environment.
>
> We are keen to identify an outgoing and resilient individual, probably aged 20–40, with a proven track record in packaged food sales and at least three years' full-time training experience. Probably with a university degree, but more importantly with the ability to convey information in an understandable and enjoyable way.
>
> You should see the position as an opportunity to develop yourself with a progressive and highly successful company. The attractive salary package will include a company car, private health insurance and relocation assistance to Sheffield. Apply . . .

You might think that a 'dynamic' sales trainer would recoil from the attitudes and clichés evident in this text matter. Read almost any page of recruitment advertisements to find the same, very old and weary phrases: 'competitive environment', 'proven track record', 'salary package' and so on. But even more important, the whole approach of this particular copy is equally tired and conventional. Happily, in contention with such a dull and uniform setting, an enlightened employer can make his own advertisements sparkle.

Let us, then, rewrite the text to see how it might be improved. First, the headline deserves some thought. Clearly the ideal candidate will be an enthusiast, whose devotion to the art of selling must be so intense that he or she will inspire and encourage the sales team. This is exactly the kind of person who welcomes a challenge, so perhaps the headline should be, 'Are you good enough to train the XYZ sales team?' After a little extra thought this might be shortened to, 'Could you train the XYZ sales team?'

Reference to packaged foods has been removed from the headline because the company's products are nationally famous, and in any case we are looking for people who know the market and will therefore need no introduction to the company and its products.

Now, having found a headline that will catch the eye of the right kind of candidates and excite their imagination, we can write much simpler body copy than the published version. See how the following draft explains the challenge, then immediately describes the

Could you train the XYZ sales team?

As you would imagine, we demand the highest selling standards to match our reputation in packaged foods.

With four colleagues, you will be responsible for developing the skills of our sales team to improve their performance in this formidable market. The training manuals and programmes are established and proven; now their contents must be expounded by a very special person, in a way that is both enjoyable and easily understood.

To succeed we believe you will need practical experience of selling packaged foods and have spent at least three years in full-time sales training. We also think you will be 40 or less, with a university degree, although you may prove us wrong.

This is a job where a true specialist can quickly make his or her name in our £1 billion-plus corporation. The salary is higher than you might expect, and you get a company car and private health insurance.

So if your talents as a sales trainer are truly exceptional, please ring Miss Blank on xxx to talk about the vacancy, or apply by letter if you prefer.

duties involved. Note, too, how the company's size is used in a positive way to attract applicants with ambition, and that reference to the 'admiration rating' is discarded because it is irrelevant.

This example illustrates the ways in which an advertisement can suggest the employer's attitudes and policies. Working in a small business has many attractions for go-ahead people: they enjoy direct access to management, may greatly influence the firm's progress and can advance their careers much faster. They must, however, be convinced that the proprietor or directors have sufficient aptitude and thrust to succeed, and since their first contact with the employer is through an advertisement, its contents and design are of special consequence.

Layout

The majority of small concerns merely write the text of a recruitment advertisement and allow the publisher to set the type in any way he thinks fit. Usually the results are unremarkable.

Your artist could, of course, prepare an eye-catching layout and supply finished artwork for despatch to the publisher, but this procedure might be too expensive if repeated regularly. The best solution is to ask him to draw a series of standard borders in various sizes, with your company name, address and perhaps a slogan or catch-line mounted in a suitable position. For very important vacancies you might ask him to supply complete typesetting, although for most he can provide just a border in the correct size. This will then be sent to the publication with the copy, a rough layout and type specification, but do allow plenty of time for the work, and insist on seeing a proof before the paper or periodical goes to press.

Two or more vacancies can also be featured in the same border, perhaps under a common headline.

By following this system you will ensure that your recruitment advertisements are always well presented and therefore studied by people who might otherwise ignore them. Remember, also, that these advertisements may be seen by your clients, customers or others whom you want to impress. Good design and copy will enhance your reputation and encourage recognition by those who may become your employees in the future.

Legislation

Finally, it is essential to observe the current legislation concerned with staff recruitment. Discrimination in favour of males, females, ethnic origins or colour is forbidden, and copy that violates the advertising codes is immediately rejected by the publishers. You will be wise, therefore, to seek their advice in doubtful cases and revise your text accordingly. Some companies include a uniform sentence in their recruitment advertisements confirming that there is no such discrimination. If you decide to use a standard border and address lines, you might deem it sensible to include a statement of this kind so that legal requirements cannot be overlooked.

Checklist

1. Have you prepared a job specification in writing?
2. For recruiting executives and specialists, did you consider and test local or regional media before booking space in national publications?
3. For recruiting specialists, have you pin-pointed other suitable areas of the UK and considered advertising in local or regional media?
4. Before booking space, did you debate the best timing and prepare advertisement copy to determine the ideal size?
5. Will your headline catch the attention of likely candidates?
6. Is your copy lively, unusual and persuasive?
7. Has your artist drawn a series of standard advertisement panels?
8. Does your advertisement copy comply with the law?

Further Reading

Industrial and Trade Advertising: Practical Advice for Small Businesses, H C Carter, M.CAM (Progress Publishing, Malletts College, Wenmouth Cross, St Neot, Liskeard, Cornwall PL14 6NN)

Relevant titles from Kogan Page

Be Your Own PR Man, Michael Bland
Direct Mail: Principles and Practice, Robin Fairlie
Getting Sales: A Practical Guide to Getting More Sales for Your Business, Richard D Smith and Ginger Dick
How to Advertise, Kenneth Roman and Jane Maas
The Industrial Market Research Handbook, Paul Hague
London Creative Listings 1985–86 (a directory of creative services and the companies which provide them)
Managing a Sales Team, Neil R Sweeney
Marketing and Sales Forecasting, Gordon Bolt
Promotion for the Professions, Ian Linton
The PR Week Marketing and PR Handbook
Successful Marketing for the Small Business, Dave Patten
You're On Next! Michael Bland

Index